AF686894

Urbit Systems Technical Journal

Copyright ©2025 ~ Urbit Systems Technical Journal and individual authors and artists. Art by ~dalhec-banler (p. viii); ~litmus-ritten (p. 46); ~tocrex-holpen (p. 98); and ~natnex-ronret (p. 154).

First paperback edition August 2025.
ISSN 2997-9137

urbitsystems.tech
groundwire.io
urbit.org

Published by West Martian Limited Company
Cheyenne, Wyoming

westmartian.com

Vol. 2, No. 1, 2025 : The Journal of Solid-State Computing

Urbit Systems Technical Journal

We have pondered the prospect of a Nock issue for some time. These articles represent a *summa computralis* in a sense, an account of decades of work in making a fundamental computational engine into a practical reality on which many people program every day. Nock is something less than a programming language, and something more than a bare Turing machine. It encodes structure through nouns, and telos through its kelvin decrement system. "Perfect" is the enemy of "good enough," and an agreed-upon standard better than an eternal search. Nock sits at the nexus of an uneasy tension between minimalism and pragmatism, yet it sits with grace.

As Urbit's development unfolds and Nockchain grows in proof power, it is incumbent upon us to preserve the technical and historical record of Nock computing and its intent. Some of the material in this issue is syndicated for posterity, like ~timluc-miptev's excellent Nock tutorial and ~barpub-tarber's description of Ax. Other articles represent the first exposition in print of major components of practical Nock evaluation, such as the history of Nock as a family of combinator calculi or Nock virtualization as a design target. (Besides Ax/Conk, we note as well Tibru, SKEW, and PLAN.) We are particularly proud to publish the description of NockPU, the first bare-metal Nock interpreter, by ~mopfel-winrux.

USTJ also expands herewith its artistic portfolio, with gratitude to ~norwyl-morlec, who produced iconic ASCII art splash pages for the preceding issues. We are privileged to feature new art by longtime Urbit-associated artists and designers ~dalhec-banler ~litmus-ritten, ~natnex-ronret, and ~tocrex-holpen.

We gratefully acknowledge our supporters, not only our readers and authors but the institutions that have made *USTJ* possible, namely our founding sponsor the Urbit Foundation, our publisher West Martian Limited, and our new sponsor Groundwire Syndicate. We particularly call out the herculean labors of the Urbit core development team from Tlon Corporation's foundation in 2013 to the present day, and the many application developers who have built on shifting sands gradually settling. This book is dedicated to your labors.

Computer science happens in the trenches. ⌘

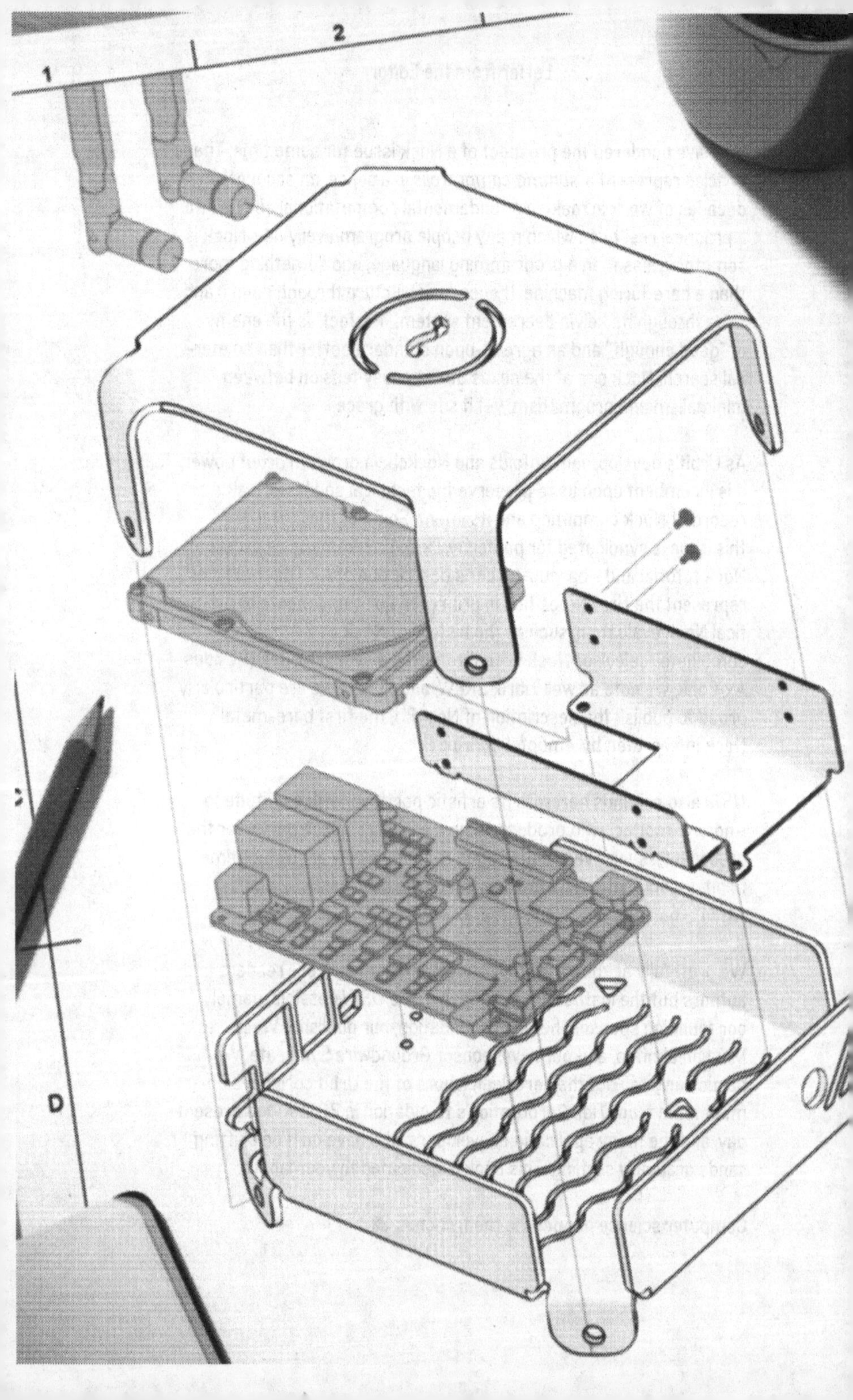
1
2
D

Nock for Everyday Coders

Tim Galebach ~timluc-miptev
Hyperware

Abstract

Nock is not super complex, and most programmers can learn the basics of it rapidly. The mental model gained by learning Nock turns out to be very useful in learning Hoon and understanding Urbit. While the Urbit docs generally suggest to not worry about Nock, Nock is very simple and small. Most programmers will feel more comfortable in Hoon having learned Nock's basics. The goal of this tutorial is to explain Nock clearly in terms most programmers will relate to, to impart a feeling of confidence with very basic Nock, and to give a knowledge of Nock's idioms and big wins so that they carry over to learning Hoon.

This tutorial was originally published online by `~timluc-miptev` in early 2020 and remains an excellent exposition of Nock's affordances.

Contents

Urbit Systems Technical Journal II:2 (2025): 1–45.
Address author correspondence to ~timluc-miptev.

1 Getting Started

When people first look at Nock, they see the definition, which is fairly intimidating. I'm talking about lines like this:

```
/[(a + a) b]          /[2 /[a b]]
```

The problem is, the programmer may already know that Nock code looks more like the below – just lists of numbers, with no symbols:

```
[6
 [5 [0 6] [1 0]]
 [0 7]
 [9 4 [[0 2] [2 [0 6] [0 5]] [4 0 7]]]
]
```

What gives? Which one is the "real" Nock?

1.1 Phases of Nock

We are looking at two different things in the examples above:

1. Pseudocode for *how to interpret* Nock.
2. Code to be interpreted (written as lists of numbers).

The symbols and spec are pseudocode, not real Nock code. They could just as easily be written in English, and they will never be written down as actual Nock code and given to an interpreter. They represent what an interpreter should do to turn Nock code into interpreter instructions.

The lists of numbers are the actual Nock code. This is what you feed to an interpreter to get some result.

1.2 What Is a Nock Interpreter?

An interpreter can be a computer program, or it can be a human manually expanding Nock code into results. In both cases, the program and human have to know the Nock pseudocode in order to do the right thing with incoming Nock code.

So a Nock interpreter is any entity that takes Nock code as input, and gives a noun as output. A noun can be:

```
:: a number
782
:: a cell (pair with two elements)
[782 9872]
:: each element can itself be a pair
```

```
[782 [9872 89728]]
:: the above can be written as
[782 9872 89728]
```

1.3 How to Run Nock Code

We will be expanding Nock pseudocode manually in the examples that follow, in effect acting as our own interpreter.

If we want to check that we're getting the right results from our manual interpretation, we need to run a Nock interpreter, such as the Urbit Dojo.

1. Start up a Dojo session on a fake ship.[1]

2. At the prompt, we can execute Nock using `.*` dottar, e.g., `.*(NOCK_SUBJECT, NOCK_FORMULA)`.

1.4 Subject, Formula?

Let's keep this simple:

- subject = an argument to a function
- formula = the function

That's it. We'll see below how this works, going really slowly with examples.

1.5 Evaluating Our First Nock Code

OK, so the interpreter takes two arguments, a "subject" and a "formula". Both are nouns (a number or a cell). Let's run some insanely simple Nock code in the Dojo:[2]

```
> .*(42 [0 1])
42
```

[1] Consult `https://docs.urbit.org` for details.

[2] Code samples beginning with › are Dojo inputs (to wit, Hoon expressions).

In the above, `42` is our subject. `[0 1]` is our formula.

Formulas are always cells, and the first element of the cell is a number that you can think of as *the name of the function.*

In this case, our function name is `0`, which is the memory slot function. It is always followed by 1 number, in this case `1`, which is the number of the memory slot to fetch in the subject.

Whenever we look at Nock code, we want to ask:

- What is the subject (function argument)? In this case, it's `42`.
- What is the formula (function)? In this case, it's `[0 1]`.
- What value does that formula (function) produce when called on this subject (argument)? In this case, the return value is `42`.

Why is the return value `42`? How does this formula work?

2 Fundamental Opcodes

2.1 Nock's Simplest Functions, `0` and `1`

The two most basic Nock functions are `0` address and `1` constant. The goal here is to get strong intuitions of what they do, how they handle edge cases, and how this relates to the Nock spec/pseudocode.

2.2 Binary Tree Addressing

Before getting started on Nock proper, we should understand how Nock and Hoon handle addresses in binary trees. If you already understand why memory slot 5 of `[['apple' %pie] [0b1101 0xdad]]` is `%pie`, you are good to go and can skip ahead to Section 2.3.

Every noun in Nock can be thought of as a tree, which means we can give an exact number to access any position in the tree. This means that, no matter how big our subject (argument) is, we can yank a value out of any part of it.

The Nock specification defines noun tree addressing:

```
/[1 a]               a
/[2 a b]             a
/[3 a b]             b
/[(a + a) b]         /[2 /[a b]]
/[(a + a + 1) b]     /[3 /[a b]]
```

This permits the address to be defined within a particular subtree as well as within the overall tree (Figure 1).

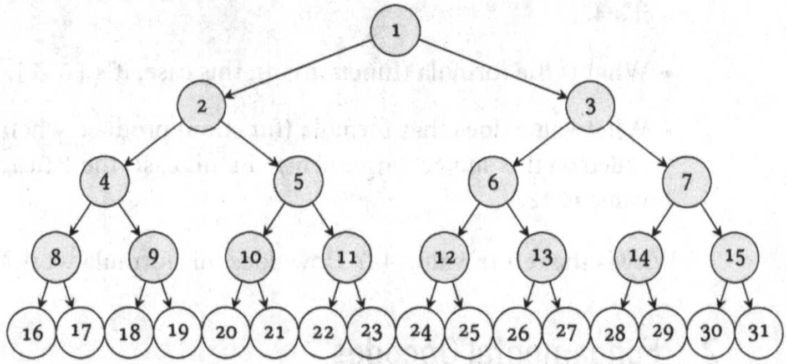

Figure 1: A binary tree with labeled node addresses to several layers.

That is, how do you say which slot number you want from a given tree? We say that:

- The tree root is address 1.
- The head of every node n is $2n$.
- The tail of every node n is $2n+1$.

Let's take an example tree to illustrate. In Nock cell form, the tree is:

```
[[4 5] [6 14 15]]
```

Diagrammatically, the tree looks like Figure 2.

- 1 is the address of the whole tree, `[[4 5] [6 14 15]]`.
- 2 is the address of the left branch, `[4 5]`.

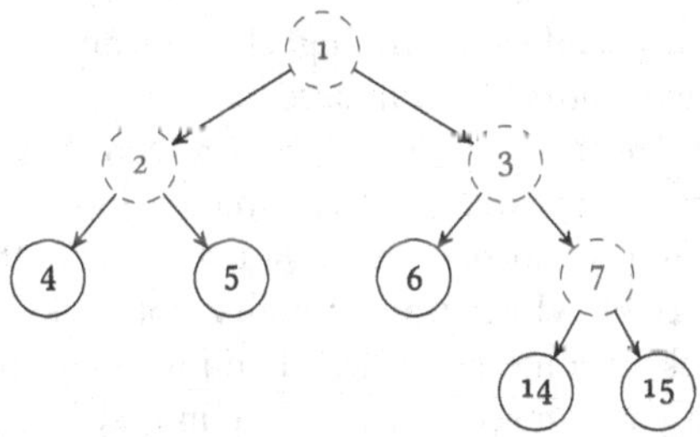

Figure 2: A binary tree with some labeled node addresses.

- 3 is the address of the right branch, `[6 14 15]`.
- 15 is the value `15`.

Let's play around now in the Dojo Nock interpreter so that we can confirm this. In each example, our subject (argument) will be the tree `[[4 5] [6 14 15]]`.

```
:: formula (function) [0 1]: get the whole tree
> .*([[4 5] [6 14 15]] [0 1])
[[4 5] 6 14 15]

:: formula (function) [0 2]: get the left branch
> .*([[4 5] [6 14 15]] [0 2])
[4 5]

:: formula (function) [0 7]: get the subtree in slot 7
> .*([[4 5] [6 14 15]] [0 7])
[14 15]
```

2.3 0, the "Memory Slot" Function

The pseudocode for the 0 opcode[3] is as follows:

```
*[a 0 b]     /[b a]
```

[3]From this point on, we will write Nock opcodes in special type so that they can be distinguished from other numbers in Nock. This reflects Hoon practice, which marks Nock rules as constants like `%0`. While not strictly necessary, it can be helpful when learning or coding Nock to see an explicit distinction.

/[b a] is pseudocode. In English, it means "a is a binary tree. Get the memory slot numbered b.

So if a were the tree [9 10], and b were 1, we'd get the memory slot 1 in the tree [9 10], which is just the tree itself.

Written in pseudocode, that's /[1 [9 10]]. We can also do /[2 [9 10]], which grabs memory slot 2, aka 9.

Let's look at some examples. I've put them first in Dojo form so that you can see how they run in that interpreter, and then I show the "human interpreter" in pseudocode below that.

2.3.1 Example: Retrieve the Subject

```
:: get memory slot 1
> .*([50 51] [0 1])
[50 51]
:: PSEUDOCODE -- replaces the Dojo's () with []
*[[50 51] [0 1]]
:: *[a 0 b] -> a = [50 51], b = 1
/[1 [50 51]]
[50 51]
```

2.3.2 Example: Retrieve the Head of the Subject

```
> .*([50 51] [0 2])
50
:: PSEUDOCODE -- replaces the Dojo's () with []
*[[50 51] [0 2]]
:: *[a 0 b] -> a = [50 51], b = 2
/[2 [50 51]]
50
```

2.3.3 Example: A Crash

```
> .*([50 51] [0 [0 1]])
dojo: hoon expression failed
:: PSEUDOCODE
*[[50 51] [0 [0 1]]]
/[[0 1] [50 51]]
```

```
:: can't evaluate this--a memory slot must be a
   number like 2, not a cell like [0 1]
CRASH
```

2.3.4 Summary of 0

0 is everywhere in Nock, because "get something from a memory slot" really means "store stuff in a place and get it whenever I want," which is another name for creating variables. These memory slot numbers take the place of variable names.

If you're familiar with assembly or C, they're conceptually similar to memory pointers or registers in how Nock uses them. Keep in mind though, Nock is functional/immutable, so it doesn't update memory locations: it creates copies of data structures with altered values.

We've also seen that the memory slot function can't take just anything as the memory slot to fetch: it must receive an atom (number).

2.4 1, the "Quoter" Function

This is another really simple function. You can think of it as a "quoter": it just returns any value passed to it exactly as it is. It ignores the subject, and just quotes the value after it. Let's look at a couple examples.

```
> .*([20 30] [1 67])
67
:: [1 2 587] is same as [1 [2 [587]]]
> .*([20 30] [1 [2 [587]])
[2 587]
```

It doesn't matter how much information is after the 1: 1 is a dumb function that just returns it all.

The pseudocode for 1 is:

```
*[a 1 b]     b
```

In English, this means: "ignore the subject a, and just return everything after the 1 exactly as it is.

Let's look at our first example, `.*([20 30] [1 67])`. The subject `a` is `[20 30]`, so we ignore that. What's after the 1? 67, so we return that.

In the second example, "everything after the 1" is longer, but the same rule applies: the Nock interpreter just returns it exactly as it is, after stripping out unnecessary brackets.

2.4.1 Summary of 1

1 is a simple function that just returns whatever is after it ("quoter" or "constant"). It's useful for quoting values that you want to use later in your Nock code.

2.5 4, the Incrementing Function

0 and 1 are simple functions that don't have any nested behavior. Now we're going to move to a function that *does* have nested children, opcode 4. In these examples, pay attention to how 4 operates on its arguments; we'll look at pseudocode and break down the examples in a moment.

```
> .*(50 [4 0 1])
51

> .*(50 [4 4 0 1])
52

> .*([100 150] [4 4 0 3])
152

> .*(50 [4 1 98])
99

> .*(50 [4 1 [0 2]])
dojo: hoon expression failed
```

Here's 4's pseudocode, juxtaposed with that of 0 and 1:

```
*[a 4 b]   +*[a b]
*[a 0 b]   /[b a]
*[a 1 b]   b
```

In English, this says "when we have subject `a`, function 4, and Nock code `b`, first evaluate `[a b]` as `[subject formula]`, and then add 1 to the result."

If we contrast with 0 and 1, we see that the right side has a `*` symbol. This symbol means "evaluate the expression again in the Nock interpreter." 0 and 1 *did not* have this symbol, and that's why they couldn't evaluate nested Nock expressions.

2.5.1 Example: Walking Through Increment

Let's start by translating the Dojo's `.*(subject formula)` to pseudocode of the form `*[a b]`, and then expand it line by line:

```
> .*(50 [4 0 1])
51
:: change to pseudocode
*[50 [4 0 1]]
:: move the 4 to the outside as +
+*[50 [0 1]]
:: expand the 0 opcode to the memory slot operator "/"
+/[1 50]
:: grabs the memory slot
+(50)
:: evaluate
51
```

The `[a b]` part of `+*[a b]` expands to:

```
[50 [0 1]]
```

OK, this we know how to handle! It's just our 0 function, and it wants the value in memory slot `1` of the subject. That's `50`.

Now we know that `*[a b]=50`, and we just have to add 1 to it (the `+` in `+*[a b]`). That is `51`, which is exactly what the interpreter gave us.

2.5.2 Example: Walking Through Increment

This one is similar, we just have an extra 4. We again start by translating the Dojo's `.*(subject formula)` to pseudocode, and then expand

```
> .*(50 [4 4 0 1])
52
*[50 [4 4 0 1]]
:: the first 4 moves outside as a '+'
+*[50 [4 0 1]]
:: 2nd 4 becomes a '+'...we have opcode 0 again!
++*[50 [0 1]]
++/[1 50]
++(50)
+(51)
52
```

2.5.3 Example: Walking Through Serial Increment

Here we again see lots of 4s applied consecutively, and we also see how we can yank values out of a more complicated subject and manipulate them. Notice how the subject is a cell, not an atom. The rest is the same as in the previous example.

```
> .*([100 150] [4 4 0 3])
152
a (the subject) = [100 150]
*[[100 150] [4 4 0 3]]
+*[[100 150] [4 0 3]]
:: Now we've extracted all the increments,
:: so we just grab the value at memory slot 3
++*[[100 150] [0 3]]
++/[3 [100 150]]
++(150)
+(151)
152
```

2.5.4 Example: Walking Through Incrementing a Constant

In the below example, we see how we can use the quote/constant function 1 to generate the value 98 and increment it. We ignore the subject 50 completely.

```
> .*(50 [4 1 98])
99
*[50 [4 1 98]]
:: formula is the "quoter" function
```

```
+*[50 [1 98]]
+(98)
99
```

2.5.5 Example: A Crash When Incrementing a Cell

Just as opcode 0 had values it couldn't handle (non-atoms), so opcode 4 needs the nested value inside it to evaluate to an atom.

```
> .*(50 [4 1 [0 2]])
dojo: hoon expression failed
*[50 [4 1 [0 2]]]
:: OK cool, the nested value is a 1 opcode
+*[50 [1 [0 2]]]
:: 1 ignores the subject (50) and just returns [0 2]
+([0 2])
:: [0 2] isn't an atom, so how can we increment it???
:: We can't, so we crash.
dojo: hoon expression failed
```

2.5.6 Summary of 4

In these examples, we've seen that function 4 can be called as many times in a row as we want. At the end of those calls, it always ends up incrementing a number that either is yanked from the subject (memory slot function 0) or quoted as it is (quote function 1).

2.6 The Cell-Maker (aka the Distribution Rule)

The Nock interpreter is allowed to return nouns, which are atoms (positive numbers) or cells (pairs of nouns). What have our functions/opcodes been returning so far?

- 0: atoms or cells, depending what's in the memory slot that we yoink.
- 1: atoms or cells, depending on what we quote.
- 4: just atoms.

But what if my subject was `[51 67 89]`, and I wanted to increment every value and return that as `[52 68 90]`? How can I do that when it's a cell, and 4 only seems able to return atoms?

The answer is something that the Nock docs call the "distribution rule" or "implicit cons" (hello, fellow Lispers!), but that I find easiest to think of as the "Cell-Maker Rule".

2.6.1 A Quick Detour into Nock Formulas

We haven't talked much yet about what values are legal to feed into the Nock interpreter (the `.*(subject formula)` function in the Dojo). So far, we've only been using formulas that start with numbers (our functions/opcodes 0/1/4).

Let's now fully solidify our understanding of what's a legal formula by taking a quick look at the three possible cases. (The format is `.*(subject formula)`.)

- The formula is a cell starting with an opcode. We know this is OK.

```
> .*(50 [0 1])
50
```

- The formula is just an atom (0). This is not valid.

```
> .*(50 0)
dojo: hoon expression failed
```

- Finally, we try a formula that is a cell starting with an atom. This looks invalid, but—it works!

```
> .*(50 [[0 1] [1 203]])
[50 203]
```

So apparently a formula cell can start with a cell. The Cell-Maker rule is:

```
*[subject [formula-x formula-y]]→
  [*[subject formula-x] *[subject formula-y]]
```

In our example above, `formula-x` is `[0 1]`, and `formula-y` is `[1 203]`. They each evaluate individually against the subject, and the end result is a cell.

We can make as many cells in a row as we want:

```
> .*(50 [[0 1] [1 203] [0 1] [1 19] [1 76]])
[50 203 50 19 76]
```

We can put any operation inside each cell:

```
> .*([19 20] [[0 1] [1 76] [4 4 0 3]])
[[19 20] 76 22]
```

If we take the returned collection `[[19 20] 76 22]` in order, we can write in English how they connect to our collection of formulas that we passed:

- `[0 1]`: get memory slot 1
- `[1 76]`: return the quoted value 76
- `[4 4 0 3]`: increment twice the value in memory slot 3 (20)

So we can pass one small subject (`[19 20]`) and make an arbitrarily long collection of values from it, using any functions we want. Cell-Maker FTW!

2.7 3, the Cell Detector, and 5, the Equality Tester

Now we come to functions/opcodes 3 and 5, which are pretty straightforward after we've seen how 4 and the Cell-Maker work. Functions 3 and 5, like 4, allow nested evaluation. Let's put all their pseudocode definitions together to compare:

```
::  function/opcode 3
*[a 3 b]     ?*[a b]
:: function/opcode 4
*[a 4 b]     +*[a b]
:: function/opcode 5
*[a 5 b c]   =[*[a b] *[a c]]
```

First of all, notice how the right side of all these "equations" has the evaluation operator, `*`. This means that these functions can have nested formulas, since they keep evaluating all the way down.

There are some new pseudocode symbols here that we need to translate into English. We already know `+`: "increment the value after this". Now we also see:

- `?`: "check whether the value after this is a cell. Return 0 if yes, 1 if no".[4]
- `=`: "first run the function in `b` with subject `a` as the argument, and same for the function in `c`. If the results are equal, return 0, if not, return 1.

2.7.1 Example: Not a Cell

```
> .*(50 [3 0 1])
1
:: PSEUDOCODE OF THE ABOVE
*[50 [3 0 1]]
?*[50 [0 1]]
::get memory slot 1 of the subject
?(50)
:: is 50 a cell? No, so return 1
1
```

2.7.2 Example: A Cell

```
> .*([50 51] [3 0 1])
0
:: PSEUDOCODE OF THE ABOVE
*[[50 51] [3 0 1]]
?*[[50 51] [0 1]]
::get memory slot 1 of the subject: [50 51]
?([50 51])
:: is [50 51] a cell? Yes, so return 0
0
```

[4] Nock conventionally explains that there is one "true" case and (potentially) many "false" cases, thus 0/`true` and 1/`false`.

2.7.3 Example: Nested Cell Evaluation with 4

```
> .*([50 51] [4 4 3 0 1])
2
:: PSEUDOCODE OF THE ABOVE
*[[50 51] [4 4 3 0 1]]
+*[[50 51] [4 3 0 1]]
:: whatever comes out of the 3 function,
:: we're gonna increment it twice
++*[[50 51] [3 0 1]]
:: down to just fetching memory slot 1
++?*[[50 51] [0 1]]
++?([50 51])
:: is [50 51] a cell? Yes, so return 0
++(0)
+(1)
2
```

2.7.4 Example: Check Multiple Cases of Cells

```
> .*([[50 51] 52] [[3 0 2] [3 0 3]])
[0 1]
*[[[50 51] 52] [[3 0 2] [3 0 3]]]
?[*[[50 51] 52] [0 2]]
   *[[50 51] [0 3]]]
:: yank memory slots 2 and 3
?*[[50 51] 52]
:: first is a cell, second is not
[0 1]
```

2.7.5 Example: Equality Test

Because 5 compares the results of 2 formulas, it *always* makes 2 inner evaluations of the subject. It's similar to Cell-Maker in this way.

```
> .*([50 51] [5 [0 2] [0 2]])
0
:: PSEUDOCODE
*[[50 51] [5 [0 2] [0 2]]]
```

```
:: factor out the =
=[*[[50 51] [0 2]] *[[50 51] [0 2]]]
:: get memory slot 2 twice
=(50 50)
0
```

2.7.6 Example: Comparing Two Unequal Values

```
> .*([50 51] [5 [0 2] [0 3]])
1
:: PSEUDOCODE
*[[50 51] [5 [0 2] [0 3]]]
:: factor out the =
=[*[[50 51] [0 2]] *[[50 51] [0 3]]]
:: get memory slot 2 and memory slot 3
=(50 51)
1
```

2.7.7 Example: Compare Values with Function Calls

```
> .*([50 51] [5 [4 0 2] [0 3]])
0
:: PSEUDOCODE
*[[50 51] [5 [4 0 2] [0 3]]]
:: factor out the =
=[*[[50 51] [4 0 2]]
   *[[50 51] [0 3]]]
:: factor out the +
=[+*[[50 51] [0 2]]
    *[[50 51] [0 3]]]
:: get memory slots 2 and 3
=[+50 51]
:: evaluate the +
=([51 51])
0
```

2.7.8 Example: Compare Cells with Function Calls

```
> .*([99 99] [5 [1 [99 99]] [0 1]])
0
:: PSEUDOCODE
*[[99 99] [5 [1 [99 99]] [0 1]]]
=[*[[99 99] [1 [99 99]]]
  *[[99 99] [0 1]]]
:: first cell is the result of quoter function
:: second cell is the result of memory fetch
=[[99 99] [99 99]]
:: true
0
```

2.7.9 Summary of 3 and 5

These along with 4 are known as the "axiomatic" functions. They exist to implement definitional logic for the Nock specification. In particular, the cell check and the equality check provide for structural analysis of nouns.

2.8 2, the "Subject-Altering" Function

In all our examples so far, the subject has been defined at the start when we call the interpreter, and never changes. But what if we want to change the subject?

A different subject? Why would we want that? Here's an easy example. Say you found the following piece of Nock code on the interwebz:

```
[8 [1 0] 8 [1 6 [5 [0 7] 4 0 6] [0 6] 9 2 [0 2]
            [4 0 6] 0 7] 9 2 0 1]
```

This is the code for a Nock function that expects a subject that is an atom, and decrements that subject by 1. You can actually enter it in the Dojo right now:

```
> .*(100 [8 [1 0] 8 [1 6 [5 [0 7] 4 0 6] [0 6] 9 2 [0
    2] [4 0 6] 0 7] 9 2 0 1])
99
```

This works! You do not have to understand the code right now; just try entering different numbers instead of `100` to see the program working.

But now imagine that I have a Nock program with a different subject

```
> .*([50 51] some-formula)
```

And somewhere inside `some-formula`, I want to decrement the number `51`. I can't pass `[50 51]` as the subject to my decrementer code above though, because that's a cell, and it expects just an atom (a number).

2.8.1 Subject Altering to the Rescue

The function/opcode 2 is designed to handle this problem for us. First the pseudocode:

```
*[a 2 b c]  *[*[a b] *[a c]]
```

2 expects 2 formulas after the subject `a`: `b` and `c`. With those, it:

1. runs formula `b` against the subject to set up a new environment/subject derived from the subject
2. runs formula `c` against the subject to prepare a 2nd function
3. run that 2nd function against the new environment/subject from step (1)

Note that the pseudocode for 2 has nested `*`s.

```
*[*[a b] *[a c]]
```

The two inner `*`s run steps (1) and (2), and the outer one, around the whole expression, runs step (3).

2.8.2 Example: Change the Subject and Call a Constant Value

```
> .*([50 51] [2 [0 3] [1 [4 0 1]]])
52
:: PSEUDOCODE
*[[50 51] [2 [0 3] [1 [4 0 1]]]]
:: separate b and c to each run against the subject
  (steps 1 and 2)
```

```
*[*[[50 51] [0 3]] *[[50 51] [1 [4 0 1]]]]
:: after steps 1 and 2, we have a new subject, 51!
:: note how we're back in normal *[subject formula]
   form
*[51 [4 0 1]]
:: apply the 4 function as we're used to
+*[51 [0 1]]
:: grab 51 from memory slot 1
+(51)
52
```

2.8.3 Example: Grab a Block of Code from the Subject and Run It

Think of this as grabbing a "stored procedure" from the subject.

```
> .*([[4 0 1] 51] [2 [0 3] [0 2]]])
52
:: PSEUDOCODE, subject is [[4 0 1] 51]
*[[[4 0 1] 51] [2 [0 3] [0 2]]]
*[*[[[4 0 1] 51] [0 3]
  *[[[4 0 1] 51] [0 2]]]]
:: step 1 gets memory slot 3, step 2 grabs memory
   slot 2
*[51 [4 0 1]]
:: looks like a normal 4 opcode to me!
+*[51 [0 1]]
:: grab memory slot 1
+(51)
52
```

2.8.4 Example: Back to Our Motivating Case

Remember our decrementing block of code that we couldn't use when the subject was `[50 51]`, instead of just an atom? Opcode 2 makes handling that issue a piece of cake.

We simply use 2 to transform our subject into an atom, and use 1 to quote the decrement block of code before it evaluates in step (3).

```
> .*([50 51] [2 [0 2] [1 [8 [1 0] 8 [1 6 [5 [0 7] 4 0
   6] [0 6] 9 2 [0 2] [4 0 6] 0 7] 9 2 0 1]]])
```

```
49
:: PSEUDOCODE (subject is [50 51])
:: ("decrement-formula" substituted for clarity)
*[[50 51] [2 [0 2] [1 decrement-formula]]]
*[*[[50 51] [0 2]] *[[50 51] [1 decrement-formula]]]
*[50 decrement-formula]
::decrement-formula has the atom subject that it wants
49
```

2.8.5 Summary of 2

For those who know a bit of Hoon, the second example above is rather similar to calling an arm that produces a gate, and then running the gate. Most of Hoon runs this type of stored-procedure plus subject-altering Nock, and it all uses opcode 2 at its base.

And for those who know Hoon, `[[4 0 1] 51]` should already be looking a lot like `[battery payload]`... that's not a coincidence. We're starting to see the first glimpses of how Hoon's cores, arms and subjects/subject mutations flow out of the fundamental structure of Nock.

We also see how Hoon/Nock lend themselves well to throwing around chunks of code, and adjusting the subject as necessary to create the correct subject/environment against which to run that code.

2.9 Summary of Fundamental Opcodes

You now have seen all the fundamental functions/opcodes in Nock. In the next part, I'll introduce the remaining functions, which no longer need pseudocode: we have enough scaffolding now to build the rest of Nock from Nock itself. Instead, these new opcodes will just be shortcuts/macros/code expansions building on opcodes 0–5.

We'll also start to connect Nock to Hoon, and see how most of the fundamental (and slightly weird) features of Hoon flow directly from Nock's structure, and make a lot more sense in combination with it.

3 Composite Opcodes

A word of encouragement: we're done with the hard part now. Every Nock function we learn in this section will be built from pieces in the preceding section.

None of these new functions are *necessary* to make Nock work. All of them except Nock 10 and 11 are syntactic sugar that is part of the Nock definition, and must be built into every correct Nock implementation. If you have seen macros or code expansions in other languages, that's another word for what's happening here.

Nock 10 makes it easier to replace a memory value somewhere in a tree, and Nock 11 allows passing hints to the interpreter.

One point of clarity: this syntactic sugar/code-expansion system is *not* extensible. This means that you can't invent your own Nock opcodes and still have that language be Nock; you're making a higher-level language on top of Nock at that point.

In fact, that's not a bad way to think of Hoon: it's a higher-level language that adds missing syntatic sugar/macros and human-readable names to Nock. (That's not the whole story, but it's a decent mental peg to initially hang Hoon on.)

Nock is intentionally very, very small, such that you can always walk through and analyze what is happening in a block of code if you know Nock's opcodes.

3.1 An Aside About the 1 (Quoter Function)

You're going to see the 1 opcode (the "Quoter") appear in a lot of examples below for a simple reason: the 6-9 opcodes expect formulas in a lot of places, not just atoms. And, as we've seen already, formulas have to be cells.

Whenever a formula is required, but you really just want to return a number, you use the quoter function.

3.1.1 Example: Incrementing a Constant

```
:: We just want to run 4 on the number 5,
```

```
:: but 4 expects a formula after it, so we use [1 5]
> .*(0 [4 1 5])
6
```

3.1.2 Example: Comparing a Memory Slot to a Constant Value

```
:: we grab memory slot 2
:: then it has to be compared to the result of a
   formula
:: so we just use the formula [1 23] to return 23
> .*([23 45] [5 [0 2] [1 23]])
0
```

3.2 6, "If/Else" Conditional Branch

The remaining Nock opcodes are "sugar". This means that the functions in this next part will use only * and Nock code in their pseudocode. For example, here is the code for 6, the "If/Else" function.

```
*[a 6 b c d]        *[a *[[c d] 0 *[[2 3] 0 *[a 4 4 b]]]]
```

The prose explanation of what's happening is straightforward:

1. Evaluate b against the subject a (*[a b]) to see whether it's 0/true or 1/false.
2. If b equals 0/true, run formula c against subject a.
3. If b equals 1/false, run formula d against subject a.
4. If b is not equal to 0 or 1, the code crashes, for reasons we'll see in the code explanation.

3.2.1 Code Explanation (Way More Fun)

OK, so that's the English version. The code explanation (the right side of the definition) is *really fun* now that we know the basic Nock opcodes.

The pseudocode has four nested `*[subject formula]`s, so I'm going to unwrap those to the bottom, and then build it up again. The layers are, in order:

1. `*[a ...]`, i.e. subject `a` evaluated against that long formula starting with `*[[c d] 0 ...]`.
2. `*[c d]`, i.e. subject `c` evaluated against the formula starting with `[[2 3 ...]`.
3. `*[2 3]`, i.e. subject `2` evaluated against the lowest-level formula.
4. Finally, subject `a` evaluated against formula `[4 4 b]`.

3.2.2 Step 4

Remember, our English explanation was "see if `*[a b]` is true or false, and do different actions depending on that. Step Four is that check.

Let's say we have `a` as `59`, and `b` as the quoted value 0/true.

```
*[a 4 4 b]
:: a: 59
:: b: [1 0]
*[59 4 4 [1 0]]
:: substitute out the two increment operators
++*[59 [1 0]]
:: ignore subject, return quoted value 0
++(0)
2
```

In summary, because `*[a b]` evaluated to 0/true, we get the number `2`. If `*[a b]` had been 1/false, we'd get `3` (because we'd evaluate `++(1)`).

What the heck? Why are we getting 2 or 3 back? How does that help us?? Well, Nock uses that returned 2 or 3 as a *memory slot*, and executes the code in that memory slot.

3.2.3 Step 3

Now we go up to step 3, with the subject `[2 3]` evaluated against our return value from step 4. Let's imagine that `2` had been returned:

```
:: remember, "result-of-step-4" was 2
*[[2 3] 0 result-of-step-4]
*[[2 3] 0 2]
:: get memory slot 2
2
```

This grabs memory slot 2 if `*[a b]` was true, and memory slot 3 if `*[a b]` was false.

Wait, isn't this redundant? We are just using our 2 or 3 generated in step 4 to generate a 2 or a 3. Seems dumb.

The answer is that we make sure that a crash happens if `*[a b]` yields any answer other than 0/true or 1/false. If `*[a b]` returned 10, for example, we'd have the following code in step 3:

```
*[[2 3] 0 10]
:: there's no slot 10
CRASH!!
```

This is exactly what we want: the program crashes unless we are doing a loobean[5] test that returns a 0 or 1 (converted to an indicial 2 or 3) in step 4.

3.2.4 Step 2

We now have our validated 2 or 3 to plug into step 2. Let's imagine `c` is the simple formula `[0 1]` and `d` is `[1 203]`.

```
:: if step 3 returned "2" (true)
*[[[0 1] [1 203]] 0 2]
[0 1]
```

Not much to see here: we just grab memory slot 2 or 3 depending on whether our initial `b` was true or false.

3.2.5 Step 1

And now we're back at the top level, where we just use whichever formula we yoinked in step 2 and run it against `a`.

[5] A boolean truth value but with the typical truth values of 0 and 1 reversed to 0/`true` and 1/`false`.

```
*[a formula-from-step-2]
:: let's say we returned formula [0 1]
:: our original a, from step 4, was 59
*[59 [0 1]]
59
```

3.2.6 Example: Code Expansion of 6

```
> .*(1 [6 [0 1] [0 1] [4 0 1]])
:: PSEUDOCODE
:: *[a *[[c d] 0 *[[2 3] 0 *[a 4 4 b]]]]
*[1 *[[[0 1] [4 0 1]] 0 *[[2 3] 0 *[1 4 4 [0 1]]]]]
:: factor out the 4 opcodes
*[1 *[[[0 1] [4 0 1]] 0 *[[2 3] 0 ++*[1 [0 1]]]]]
:: b evaluates to 1 (yank memory slot 1)
*[1 *[[[0 1] [4 0 1]] 0 *[[2 3] 0 ++(1)]]]
:: evaluate the two increments
*[1 *[[[0 1] [4 0 1]] 0 *[[2 3] 0 3]]]
:: get memory slot 3 from [2 3]
*[1 *[[[0 1] [4 0 1]] 0 3]]
:: [0 3] means get memory slot 3 from the subject
    (formula [4 0 1])
*[1 [4 0 1]]
:: factor out the 4 opcode
+*[1 [0 1]]
+(1)
2
```

3.2.7 Summary of 6

Now I'm going to make you a little sad. Most Nock interpreters don't do this whole awesome code expansion. They just see 6, and implement an if/else check with a crash if `*[a b]` isn't a loobean.

However, the pattern of storing chunks of code in memory and pulling them out when you want them is the most important part of Nock. In fact, those of you who know Hoon are probably already seeing the makings of the "core" code pattern.

3.3 7, the "Composition" Opcode

7 is so simple we barely need to spend time on it. All it does is create a new subject/environment (using 2), and immediately runs a formula against that new subject. Let's compare it to 2:

```
::opcode 7
*[a 7 b c]  *[*[a b] c]

:: opcode 2
*[a 2 b c]  *[*[a b] *[a c]]
```

This is almost exactly the same except with `c` instead of `*[a c]`. This means that you can write a "subject-changing" formula in `b`, and then run a simple function against that in `c`.

3.3.1 Example: Opcode 2 vs. Opcode 7

```
:: using opcode 2
> .*([23 45] [2 [0 3] [1 4 0 1]])
46

:: using opcode 7 -- we get to remove the quoter
   opcode "1"
:: wow amazing /sarcasm
> .*([23 45] [7 [0 3] [4 0 1]])
46
```

Opcode 7 is clearly trivial, so why does it exist? It allows clean expression of function composition: this is really `c(b(a))`, where `a` (the subject) is the initial argument, and `b` and `c` are functions. This pattern comes up a ton, and it's nice to not use 1s everywhere.

3.4 8, the "Variable Push" Opcode

If you're ever writing Nock and think "how can I add a new variable to the subject?", opcode 8 is what you want. The new variable can be based on either the existing subject, or be a new value you add on.

```
*[a 8 b c]            *[[*[a b] a] c]
```

This says to run `*[a b]`, and then make that the head of a new subject, with the old subject `a` as the new subject's tail.

3.4.1 Example: Add Variable as a Copied Value from an Existing Subject

In English, the below code first yanks the variable from memory slot 3, copies it to the head of a new subject, and then increments the value in that new head.

```
> .*([67 39] [8 [0 3] [4 0 2]])
40
:: PSEUDOCODE
*[[*[[67 39] [0 3]] [67 39]] [4 0 2]]
:: yanks mem slot 3 and pins it to the front of the old subject
*[[39 [67 39]] [4 0 2]]
+*[[39 [67 39]] [0 2]]
+(39)
40
```

3.4.2 Example: Add Variable as a New Value

```
> .*([67 39] [8 [1 0] [4 0 2]])
1
:: PSEUDOCODE
*[[*[[67 39] [1 0]] [67 39]] [4 0 2]]
*[[0 [67 39]] [4 0 2]]
+*[[0 [67 39]] [0 2]]
+(0)
1
```

Why do we want this? In the first example, we pin a copy of a value so that we can manipulate it without changing the original. In the second example, we add a `0` to the front; maybe we want to increment it until some condition is met?

The above should be starting to feel *very* Hoon-ish: we're a minor code transform away from pinning new values to the head of a payload.

3.5 9, Run a Stored Procedure Arm in a Core

We're almost at full Hoon now, although still at a very low/raw level. 9 looks a little complicated...

```
*[a 9 b c]  *[*[a c] 2 [0 1] 0 b]
```

... but in English, this is just saying:

1. Use formula `c` to make a new subject from `a` (`*[a c]`).
2. Grab the formula located at memory slot `b` in that new subject.
3. Run that formula against the new subject `*[a c]`.

The fact that the above description has the words "make a new subject" tells us right away that it's syntactic sugar for opcode 2, and that's indeed what we see in the pseudocode.

3.5.1 Example: Using 9 to Run an Increment Arm

The initial expression here likely looks cryptic, but if you follow the pseudocode, it will become clear.

To stay oriented, remember that, if we're thinking of 9 as `*[a 9 b c]`, then

```
a: 45
b: 2
c: [[1 4 0 3] 0 1]
```

```
> .*(45 [9 2 [1 4 0 3] 0 1])
46
:: PSEUDOCODE
*[45 [9 2 [1 4 0 3] [0 1]]]
*[*[45 [1 4 0 3] [0 1]] 2 [0 1] 0 2]
:: new subject is [[4 0 3] 45]
:: that is a formula to increment mem slot 3 in the
:: head; 45 in the tail
*[[[4 0 3] 45] 2 [0 1] 0 2]
:: now we expand opcode 2
*[*[[[4 0 3] 45] 0 1]
  *[[[4 0 3] 45] 0 2]]
```

```
:: mem slot 2 of the subject becomes the new formula
*[[[4 0 3] 45] 4 0 3]
+*[[[4 0 3] 45] 0 3]
:: grab mem slot 3
+(45)
46
```

We start above with a subject that is not a core; it's just the atom 45. The code for `c` is then:

```
[[1 4 0 3] [0 1]]
```

This formula uses the Cell Maker (Distribution Rule) to insert `[4 0 3]` as the head of the new subject, and puts mem slot 1 of the old subject as the tail, so we get a new subject of `[[4 0 3] 45]`.

What we do next is use `b` (here, 2) to select memory slot 2 from that new subject. Memory slot 2 is a formula: `[4 0 3]`. We run that formula against the new subject.

3.5.2 Key Point/Possible Confusion

When I first saw 9, I thought: "why didn't they just use 2 to make the transformed subject? Why is there an extra step to use `[0 1]` to pull the new `*[a c]` subject? Why can't we do `*[a 2 c [0 b]]`?

The answer is that we actually use the `*[a c]` subject *twice*:

1. We extract from it the formula located at memory slot `b`.
2. Then we run *that* formula against the `*[a c]` subject.

If we just did `*[a 2 c [0 b]]`, then `[0 b]` would try to look up the `b` memory slot in `a`, NOT `*[a c]`. So 9 gives us one extra step to set up the core itself.

3.5.3 How to Think of 9

I like to think of 9 as having three parts:

1. `c`: our formula to set up the subject, making a new subject.

2. b: the memory slot in our new subject where an arm is.

3. Run the arm located at b against the new subject.

You can think of this as setting up a subject, pulling a stored procedure from it, and then running that procedure against the subject.

3.6 10, Replace a Memory Slot

Before explaining 10, we need to introduce a new operator, # hax. # hax is the "edit" operator. It has the form

```
#[mem-slot new-val target-tree]
```

It replaces the memory slot `mem-slot` in `target-tree` with `new-val`.

```
::  Example
#[2 [4 5] [99 88 77]]
[[4 5] 88 77]
```

The pseudocode for 10 is:

```
*[a 10 [b c] d]  #[b *[a c] *[a d]]
```

In English, this first calculates `*[a c]` and `*[a d]`, and then replaces memory slot b in the latter with the result of the former.

3.6.1 Example: Using 10 to Replace a Memory Slot

```
> .*(50 [10 [2 [0 1]] [1 8 9 10]])
[50 9 10]
::  PSEUDOCODE
*[50 [10 [2 [0 1]] [1 8 9 10]]]
#[2 *[50 0 1] *[50 1 8 9 10]]
#[2 /[1 50] [8 9 10]]
#[2 50 [8 9 10]]
::  expanded as far as we can, now do the edit
::  replace mem slot 2 of [8 9 10] with the value 50
[50 9 10]
```

We will defer discussion of opcode 11 to a later section because it is not part of strict Nock semantics.

3.6.2 Towards Hoon

If "grab a chunk of code from a subject and then run it against the subject" sounds a lot like getting an arm from a core in Hoon, that's because it is. Nock opcode 9 is hand-in-glove with Hoon's core/arm structure. The "new subjects" created by `*[a c]` are cores, and the things selected from memory slots by `b` are arms.

3.7 Real Nock Code

To finish this off and take your new powers for a spin, let's look at some real Nock code from the wild. I got the below example from the Dojo. It's a mold: a function that takes a noun and returns it if it's the correct type, and crashes if not. The mold here checks whether the input noun is a loobean (`0`/true or `1`/false).

3.7.1 Example: A Loobean Mold

```
:: loobean mold gate
> =loobean-mold ?

:: below output truncated for our purposes here
> loobean-mold
< 1.fxf ... >

::  grab the code for the battery
> -.loobean-mold
[8 [6 [5 [1 0] 0 6] [1 0] 6 [5 [1 1] 0 6] [1 1] 0 0]
 8 [5 [0 14] 0 2] 0 6]
```

So we:

1. Assign the mold gate denoted by ? to the face `loobean-mold`.
2. Examine what's inside, seeing that the head is an arm.
3. Print out that source code by calling the head.

The below code acts as a formula which evaluates its sample, and returns it if it's a loobean or crashes otherwise. Let's see how that works.

```
[6 [5 [1 0] 0 6] [1 0] 6 [5 [1 1] 0 6] [1 1] 0 0]
```

We start with 6, which means this is an if-else. The true/false test is the next element:

```
[5 [1 0] 0 6]
```

This compares the quoted value `0` (from `[1 0]`) with the value at memory slot `6` in the subject (`[0 6]`).

What is the subject and what is at mem slot `6`? This code is the arm of a gate, so the subject is that gate/core: `[battery [sample payload]]`. We are looking at the battery right now, and so `[0 6]` yanks the head of the tail, or the `sample`!

We know the sample will be a noun that we're testing for loobeanness, so this code starts by seeing whether the sample is the value `0`/true. If it is, the next element is `[1 0]`, so we return `0` if the sample is `0`.

Otherwise, we run the second branch of the `if-else` conditional:

```
[6 [5 [1 1] 0 6] [1 1] 0 0]
```

This is also an opcode 6 if-else. Once again, it compares something to the value at mem slot `6` (the sample), but this time it checks whether that is the value `1`. If it is, it runs the formula `[1 1]` to return `1`.

If not, it means our input was neither `0` nor `1` and is not a loobean, so we run the formula `[0 0]`, which always crashes (as there is no memory slot `0`).[6] This is exactly what we want—crash if the sample is not a loobean!

The second part of the formula which is composed with an 8 is:

```
[8 [5 [0 14] 0 2] 0 6]
```

This checks whether the battery of the current gate is equivalent to the head of the context; if so, it returns the sample. This

[6] Recall that in the binary tree addressing scheme of Nock, 1 refers to the entire noun, 2 to its head if it exists, and 3 to its tail if it exists.

is a artifact of a type promotion in Hoon which converts a bare loobean value to a constant by pinning a constant as an example first (i.e., at slot 14). (It's completely extraneous in Nock itself, however.)

3.8 Summary

In this section, we've seen how to use almost all of the remaining opcodes, which build Nock up to a slightly more expressive level. We also saw how Hoon cores start to arise pretty naturally out of the Nock primitives, especially 8 and 9. Then we walked through real production Nock code to show that everything we've learned so far works exactly as expected in the wild. In the next section, you'll learn how to write real programs in Nock, and compose those programs to make new ones. Finally, hopefully you now see that, whatever its other limitations, Nock is not particularly obscurantist, and is fairly straightforward to parse, once you understand its syntax and idioms.

4 Interlude

In this section, we cover some loose ends deriving from the previous discussion.

4.1 Order of Operations

At this point, we can answer the question of what order Nock evaluates expressions in. The answer is straightforward: it starts with code that has only one pseudocode operator and all Nock code, as below:

```
*[50 4 4 [5 [0 1] [1 50]]]
```

The interpreter can then be thought of as moving left-to-right, expanding according to its rules, until it can't expand any further into pseudocode:

```
*[50 4 4 [5 [0 1] [1 50]]]
+*[50 4 [5 [0 1] [1 50]]]
```

```
++*[50 5 [0 1] [1 50]]
++=[*[50 [0 1]] *[50 [1 50]]]
++=[/[1 50] 50]
```

Once we get to that last line, `++=[/[1 50] *[50 [1 50]]]`, no further expansion into pseudocode is possible.

At this point, the interpreter expands "inside-out", starting from the deepest operators. In this case, those are `/[1 50]` and `50`, so it does those:

```
++=[50 50]
```

Then it moves to the next-furthest-inside operator: `=`, and then to the `+` operators:

```
++=[50 50]
++(0)
+(1)
2
```

4.1.1 Summary of Nock Order of Operations

1. On the first pass, when we have Nock code `*(nock-code)`, we expand left-to-right into pseudocode.
2. On the second pass, when we've fully expanded pseudocode, we evaluate operators from the inside-out.

4.2 11, Hints and Side Effects for the Interpreter

Opcode 11 lets you compute side effects and pass information to Nock's interpreter, for that interpreter to do what it wants. The most common uses are things like jets and debugging prints. In theory, this opcode is fairly dangerous, since it tells the interpreter that it's free to do anything.

There are two different versions of 11, depending on whether the head following 11 is an atom or a cell

```
:: head is an atom (b)
*[a 11 b c]  *[a c]

:: head is a cell ([b c])
*[a 11 [b c] d]     *[[*[a c] *[a d]] 0 3]
```

This pseudocode lets 11 handle two separate use cases:

1. We just want the interpreter to process a message in its own language/environment.
2. We want the interpreter to compute some Nock code with Nock semantics before processing the hint.

4.2.1 Option #1: Interpreter Processes a Message

Imagine the following Nock:

```
.*([50 51] [11 369 0 2])
```

This passes the value 369 to the interpreter, where maybe it would be the key in a hashmap. The value associated with the could be the function to debug print the whole operation. Or the value could be a jet function that specifically knows how to compute the 0 opcode faster when it's followed by a 2.

After the interpreter does whatever, it needs to then discard the value 292.989, and computes

```
> .*([50 51] [0 2])
50
```

4.2.2 Option #2: Run Nock Code and then Process a Message

In this case, instead of passing a static value to the interpreter, we pass it a Nock computation against the subject. The result of that computation will then be available to the interpreter to use as a message.

4.2.3 Practical Use of 11: Jet Registration

Jet registration in Hoon usually looks like this:

```
++  my-function
  ~/  %my-function
  |=  var=*
  ...
```

The Hoon rune ~/ fassig uses Nock 11 to pass the value %my-function to the interpreter, where it is associated with the C code that produces the product of my-function.

4.3 Nock in Hoon

In Hoon, you can acquire the Nock code for any function by using the `!=` zaptis rune. Since this produces Nock code complete with gate calls, you may also find it helpful to cast a data type as a noun using `^-    *`, which will show you the raw Nock code for that value.

As you have seen, you can also evaluate raw Nock using the `.*` dottar rune, which evaluates to Nock opcode 2. Other Nock runes in Hoon include `.+` dotlus, which is opcode 4; `.=` dottis, which is opcode 5; and `.?` dotwut, which is opcode 3. Fake opcode 12 is not actually Nock, but is used in a virtualization context to resolve values that may not be available in the current subject.

5 The Core as Design Pattern

At this point, you now know everything there is to know about Nock syntax and basic code manipulation. However, if I asked you to go write a simple program in Nock, you'd probably have a hard time getting started. It's really helpful to see some examples of how Nock programs are designed and patterns that tend to recur in them.

We can set variables to formulas in the Urbit Dojo. We will use that in this lesson to make code easy to follow, and to show how Nock programs are made out of discrete chunks.

```
> =increment-formula [4 0 1]
> .*(50 increment-formula)
51
> =increment-formula
```

5.1 Building a Core Manually

Every Nock program is just a formula that takes in a subject (argument). In order to run full programs against a subject, we follow the following pattern:

1. First pass: set up the dominos inside an opcode like 2 (or 7/8/9). This will create a core, and evaluate it on the second pass.
2. Second pass: evaluate that core to get our result.

The pseudocode for opcode 2, this looks like:

```
*[subject 2 core-formula call-formula]
```

Almost always, however, we'll use the 9 opcode (which is sugar on top of 2) to actually start our programs running, since it supports the concept of "cores" and "arms" very naturally. (For those who know Hoon, this "set up a core and run it" pattern should feel similar to `|^` or `=>`.)

5.1.1 Example: A Simple Increment Gate

Let's take code to increment the subject and turn it into a Hoon-style gate (a core with one arm and a sample). The code itself is simple: `[4 0 1]`.

Our code expects the subject to be an atom, but Hoon gates expect their subject to be the gate itself, which has the form `[battery payload]`. So we need to adjust our formula to accept this subject format.

```
> =inc [7 [0 3] [4 0 1]]
::  verify that it increments value in the subject's
    tail (payload)
> .*([1 74] inc)
75
```

We put our formula in the head, and put a default ("bunted") sample of `0` as the payload.

```
> =inc-gate [inc 0]
> inc-gate
[[7 [0 3] 4 0 1] 0]
```

Arms are best invoked using the 9 opcode. Here we use the "standard" version of it: `[9 2 0 1]`. Recall that 9 is `*[a 9 b c]`, where `c` is the "new subject" formula, and `b` is the memory slot of that new subject to take an arm from. Here we use `[0 1]` to keep our subject (the gate) unchanged.

```
> .*(inc-gate [9 2 0 1])
1
```

To "pass a parameter" to our gate, we use the 10 op-code to edit the subject (the `inc-gate` core) and replace the payload with a value. We make our subject `[inc-gate val-to-increment]`:

```
:: notice how opcode 10 can replace the last element
   of inc-gate
::the tail of inc-gate was 0; now it's 36
> .*([inc-gate 36] [10 [3 [0 3]] 0 2])
[[7 [0 3] 4 0 1] 36]

::  now use that to set up the subject with a new
    tail (sample)
::  and call arm in memory slot 2 (our increment
    formula)
> .*([inc-gate 36] [9 2 10 [3 [0 3]] 0 2])
37
> .*([inc-gate 562] [9 2 10 [3 [0 3]] 0 2])
563
```

5.1.2 Summary

What was the point of this? We took a perfectly good increment formula that worked on atoms, and made it more complicated for the same result. Lame!

In fact, however, this setup will come in really handy when we have multiple arms in our core, not just one. We've made it easy to set up a clean environment for increment to find its sample in, no matter what other data is present. This will come in *very* handy in our third example program.

First, however, let's look at putting a more complicated formula inside a gate. (Hint: the process is the same).

5.1.3 Example: A Decrement Gate

Here we take a piece of code that decrements the subject when the subject is an atom, and turn it into a gate. For now, we will take it as a given that the decrement function given below works. (The code will crash when the input is a cell or 0)

```
::  the code: set a Dojo face =dec
> =dec [6 [5 [0 1] [1 0]] [0 0] [6 [3 0 1] [0 0] [8
    [1 0] 8 [1 6 [5 [0 7] 4 0 6] [0 6] 9 2 [0 2] [4 0
    6] 0 7] 9 2 0 1]]]

::  testing in the Dojo
> .*(100 dec)
99

:: with non-atom input we crash
.*([100 101] dec)
dojo: hoon expression failed
```

Let's re-jigger the decrement formula to accept the subject in format `[battery payload]`:

```
::  gets value in mem slot 3 and applies the
    decrement formula to it
> =dec-arm [7 [0 3] dec]

::  verify that dec-arm decrements the value in the
    tail
> .*([1 88] dec-arm)
87

::  output the full dec-arm formula code
> dec-arm
[7 [0 3] 6 [5 [0 1] 1 0] [0 0] 6 [3 0 1] [0 0] 8 [1
    0] 8 [1 6 [5 [0 7] 4 0 6] [0 6] 9 2 [0 2] [4 0 6]
    0 7] 9 2 0 1]
```

Next, assemble the core:

```
:: all we need to do is add the sample! (we give it a
    default value of 0)
> =dec-gate [dec-arm 0]
> dec-gate
[[7 [0 3] 6 [5 [0 1] 1 0] [0 0] 6 [3 0 1] [0 0] 8 [1
    0] 8 [1 6 [5 [0 7] 4 0 6] [0 6] 9 2 [0 2] [4 0 6]
    0 7] 9 2 0 1] 0]
```

```
[[7 [0 3] 6 [5 [0 1] 1 0] [0 0] 6 [3 0 1] [0 0] 8 [1
    0] 8 [1 6 [5 [0 7] 4 0 6] [0 6] 9 2 [0 2] [4 0 6]
    0 7] 9 2 0 1] 0]
```

As in the first example, we use the 10 opcode to edit the subject (the `dec-gate` core) and replace the payload with a value. We make our subject `[dec-gate val-to-decrement]`.

```
::  confirm that our 10 code places 36 in the tail
> .*([dec-gate 36] [10 [3 [0 3]] 0 2])
[[7 [0 3] 6 [5 [0 1] 1 0] [0 0] 6 [3 0 1] [0 0] 8 [1
    0] 8 [1 6 [5 [0 7] 4 0 6] [0 6] 9 2 [0 2] [4 0 6]
    0 7] 9 2 0 1] 36]

::  now use that to set up the subject with a new
::  tail (sample) and call arm in memory slot 2
::  (our decrement formula)
> .*([dec-gate 36] [9 2 10 [3 [0 3]] 0 2])
35
> .*([dec-gate 562] [9 2 10 [3 [0 3]] 0 2])
561
```

5.1.4 Example: Comparing Two Numbers

In this example we will build a Nock core that compares two numbers and returns whether they are greater than, less than, or equal to each other.

The program specification is to take two numbers `a` and `b` and return:

- `0` if `a==b`.
- `1` if `a>b`.
- `2` if `a<b`.

The trick is that the only mathematical operators we have for this are the 4 opcode for increment, 5 for equals, and a decrement Nock function that we will supply. The basic algorithm is:

- If `a==b`, return `0`.
- If `a==0`, return `2`. (I.e, `a<b`).
- If `b==0`, return `1`. (I.e., `a>b`).
- Recur with `a` and `b` both decremented.

The above works because if `a` is smaller than `b`, it hits o first. If `b` is smaller than a, it hits `0` first. If they are equal, we never decrement in the first place, so there are no issues with numbers going negative.

We will construct a core that has two arms: one arm with the algorithm logic, and a second arm with the decrement gate from the second example. These arms will live in the head of the core (think "battery").

We will put our variables `a` and `b` in the tail of the core (think "payload"). They will be updated before the core is called each time. (This is similar to a trap or door in Hoon).

The final core we will create will have the structure `[battery payload]`, which can be broken down as:

```
[[main-logic dec-gate] a b]
```

Once the core is set up, we'll invoke the algorithm logic arm to set it running. We will build the main logic "inside-out", by first defining the "recur" code, and then inserting it into our if/else tests that implement the algorithm.

This recursion logic assumes the decrement gate lives in the tail of the battery (the battery is the head), i.e. `[0 5]`. We are using `[10 [3 [0 memory-slot]] 0 5]` to extract the decrement gate from our core, and then we invoke it with `[9 2 ...]`.

This is identical to what we did in the second example—the only difference is that we now do it twice: once for memory slot 6 (`a`) and again for memory slot 7 (`b`).

```
> =dec-a [9 2 10 [3 [0 6]] 0 5]
> =dec-b [9 2 10 [3 [0 7]] 0 5]
```

```
::  we can test our formulas by making a
::  dummy core (a = 33, b = 77)
```

```
::  first formula in battery just returns
::  the current subject
> =dummy-core [[[0 1] dec-gate] 33 77]
> .*(dummy-core dec-a)
32
> .*(dummy-core dec-b)
76
```

The recursion formula here operates by invoking its subject—itself—and applying the `dec-a` and `dec-b` formulas to it. Then we use opcode 9 for the new subject's setup: replace `payload` with new `a` and `b` run the current core

```
> =recur [9 4 [[0 2] dec-a dec-b]]

:: test it -- we want to see same battery,
:: with payload being replaced with 32 and 76
> .*(dummy-core recur)
[[[0 1] [7 [0 3] 6 [5 [0 1] 1 0] [0 0] 6 [3 0 1] [0
    0] 8 [1 0] 8 [1 6 [5 [0 7] 4 0 6] [0 6] 9 2 [0 2]
    [4 0 6] 0 7] 9 2 0 1] 0] 32 76]

::  clean up the dummy-core
> =dummy-core
```

The main logic is then:

```
::  check whether a is 0; return 2 if true
::  else check whether b is 0; return 1 if true
::  else recur
> =main-logic [6 [5 [0 6] [1 0]] [1 2] [6 [5 [0 7] [1
    0]] [1 1] recur]]

::  test (we aren't doing the equality case here)
::  a < b
> .*([[main-logic dec-gate] 9 10] [9 4 0 1])
2
::  a > b
> .*([[main-logic dec-gate] 10 9] [9 4 0 1])
1
```

We build an outer test for whether `a==b`, and then if it's not, we use the 1 opcode to return the core.

```
> =battery [main-logic dec-gate]

:: payload for our core is memory slots 2 and 3 (a
   and b)
> =comparison [6 [5 [0 2] [0 3]] [1 0] [9 4 [[1
   battery] [0 2] 0 3]]]

:: test our 3 cases
> .*([0 8] comparison)
2
> .*([0 0] comparison)
0
> .*([8 0] comparison)
1
```

We can take this code and use it *anywhere* that our subject is a cell of two numbers, and it will "just work".

```
[6 [5 [0 2] 0 3] [1 0] 9 4 [1 [6 [5 [0 6] 1 0] [1 2]
   6 [5 [0 7] 1 0] [1 1] 9 4 [0 2] [9 2 10 [3 0 6] 0
   5] 9 2 10 [3 0 7] 0 5] [7 [0 3] 6 [5 [0 1] 1 0]
   [0 0] 6 [3 0 1] [0 0] 8 [1 0] 8 [1 6 [5 [0 7] 4 0
   6] [0 6] 9 2 [0 2] [4 0 6] 0 7] 9 2 0 1] 0] [0 2]
   0 3]
```

One common convention used in languages like Hoon is to denote Nock rules as constants, e.g. `%0` (corresponding to our `0`). This makes it much more straightforward to interpret hand-rolled Nock code with addresses and constants present.

6 Conclusion

After this tutorial, you should be prepared to interpret Nock code when it is produced by Hoon. Although there is only rarely any call to write Nock code directly, you should now have a good understanding of how to read and interpret it. As you write your own interpreters in the future, you may even have call to hand-roll Nock expressions on occasion.

The Alchymist, in Search of the Calm Computus, Discovers Urbit,
and prays for the successful Conclusion of his Poasting,
as was the custom of the Ancient Chymical Astrologers

Deriving Nock Opcodes 6–11

Thomas Lindstrom-Vautrin ~niblyx-malnus
Groundwire Syndicate

Abstract

Since Nock opcodes 0 through 5 are Turing complete, it should be possible to derive the operations of the remaining opcodes 6 through 11 from them. In this article, we expound on this idea and provides a detailed derivation of each opcode.

Contents

Urbit Systems Technical Journal II:2 (2025): 47–70.
Address author correspondence to ~niblyx-malnus.

1 Motivation

It is a fun exercise when learning Nock to try to derive opcodes 6 through 11 with opcodes 0 through 5. We know (or suspect) that this is possible since Nocks 0 through 5 are billed as a Turing-complete ruleset. In fact, Nocks 6 through 9 and Nock 11 are quite trivial (of these, Nock 6 is the most involved) since they are defined in terms of the * tar expression evaluator and Nocks 0 through 5. It is still instructive to write these entirely as nouns which can be evaluated against some subject using the Hoon .* dottar rune. (In the following, take `*[a ^]` to be the same as `.*(a ^)`.)

Nock 10 is not expressed in this way, however. It is expressed in terms of the # hax edit operator:

```
*[a 10 [b c] d] ==  #[b *[a c] *[a d]]
```

While opcode 10 was introduced in the decrement from Nock 5K to Nock 4K, it is still fundamentally based on the principles established by the earlier opcodes. Ultimately, we can express # hax in terms of opcodes 0 through 5, but we will find that it is not trivial. In fact, we have a hint as to how to do so in the definition of the # hax edit operator.

```
#[1 a b] ============ a
#[(a + a) b c] ====== #[a [b /[(a + a + 1) c]] c]
#[(a + a + 1) b c] == #[a [/[(a + a) c] b] c]
```

The # hax edit operator is defined in terms of the / fas slot operator, whose effect we can reproduce with base Nock opcodes using Nock 0. As long as we have a way to keep track of whether `a` is odd or even, we should be able to write this code in simple Nock. We will use this insight to create our own Nock 10 from scratch.

This process will be easier using Nock opcodes 6, 7, 8, and 9, however. So let us convince ourselves that these can be expressed as nouns composed of only Nocks 0 through 5.

2 Deriving Opcode 7

We will start with Nock 7 because it is the easiest:[1]

```
*[a 7 b c] == *[*[a b] c]
```

which looks a lot like Nock 2:

```
*[a 2 b c] == *[*[a b] *[a c]]
```

In fact, opcode 7 is basically just a glorified Nock 2 in order to allow for more direct function composition. We can easily see that if we replace our `c` from Nock 2 with a `[1 c]` we get:

```
*[a 2 b 1 c] == *[*[a b] *[a 1 c]] == *[*[a b] c]
```

Therefore `*[a 7 b c]` and `*[a 2 b 1 c]` are equivalent.

Nock 7 Primitive Equivalent

```
*[a 7 b c] == *[a 2 b 1 c]
```

3 Deriving Opcode 8

Nock 8 is also fairly straightforward.

```
*[a 8 b c] == *[[*[a b] a] c]
```

This extends the noun by pinning another noun `*[a b]` to its head, and then runs a formula `c` on this new noun. We notice two things here. One is function composition. First we add a noun to the head. Then we apply a formula to the new noun. This suggests Nock 7 and thus Nock 2. We also notice the creation of a cell from two nouns.

Recall the rule:

```
*[a [b c] d] == [*[a b c] *[a d]]
```

[1]I use `==` and `:=` as equality and assignment operators, respectively, which are not to be confused with Hoon runes or terminators.

`[*[a b] a]` can be rewritten `[*[a b] *[a 0 1]]` which can be rewritten as `*[a b 0 1]`.

By substituting back into our original formula we get:

```
*[[*[a b] a] c] ==
  *[*[a b 0 1] c] ==
  *[a 7 [b 0 1] c] ==
  *[a 2 [b 0 1] 1 c]
```

Nock 8 Primitive Equivalent

```
*[a 8 b c] == *[a 2 [b 0 1] 1 c]
```

4 Deriving Opcode 9

Nock 9 is the "function invocation" opcode. It performs some function `c` on the subject `a` and then extracts the function at slot `b` from this new subject and runs that function against that same new subject.

```
*[a 9 b c] == *[*[a c] 2 [0 1] 0 b]
```

Much of the work here is already done for us. We have a formula `[2 [0 1] 0 b]` being applied to the result of a formula `c` being applied to subject `a`. This is just Nock 7 `*[a 7 c 2 [0 1] 0 b]` which is just Nock 2 `*[a 2 c 1 2 [0 1] 0 b]`.

Nock 9 Primitive Equivalent

```
*[a 9 b c] == *[a 2 c 1 2 [0 1] 0 b]
```

As an aside, we can note that the Nock 9 is defined in terms of a combination of pseudocode operators and Nock opcodes. We can also go the other way to see what Nock 9 looks like in pure pseudocode operators.

```
*[a 9 b c]
== *[*[a c] 2 [0 1] 0 b]
== *[*[*[a c] 0 1] *[*[a c] 0 b]]
== *[*[a c] /[b *[a c]]]
```

Nock 9 Pseudocode Operator Equivalent

```
*[a 9 b c] == *[*[a c] /[b *[a c]]]
```

5 Deriving Opcode 6

Of all the opcodes so far, Nock 6 is the most complex. It is the if-then-else operator in Nock. It takes a function `b` which computes a loobean `*[a b]` on subject `a` and returns `*[a c]` if the loobean is yes (`0`) and `*[a d]` if the loobean is no (`1`).

```
*[a 6 b c d] == *[a *[[c d] 0 *[[2 3] 0 *[a 4 4 b]]]]
```

Instead of working backwards from this formula, let's derive it ourselves. First, let's select `c` or `d` from a cell `[c d]` based on whether `*[a b]` is `0` or `1`. If `*[a b]` is `0` we want to slot into the head of `[c d]` at address 2 and if `*[a b]` is `1` we want to slot into the tail of `[c d]` at address `3`. With `*[a 4 4 b] == ++*[a b]` we get address `2` from loobean `0` and address `3` from loobean `1`. To slot into `[c d]` let's simply do `*[[c d] 0 *[a 4 4 b]]`. This gives us either `c` or `d` which we then want to apply to `a`:

```
*[a *[[c d] 0 *[[a 4 4 b]]]]
```

We are almost there, but where does the `*[2 3] 0 *[a 4 4 b]` come from? Isn't slotting into `[2 3]` with `2` or `3` from `*[a 4 4 b]` redundant? We get the same value back. However, if for some reason `*[a b]` is not a loobean but is still an atom, meaning it is an integer greater than `1` and if `[c d]` is a noun with many nested cells, `*[a 4 4 b]` will return an address greater than `3` which could still be a valid address. `*[[2 3] 0 *[a 4 4 b]]` forces this to return either `2` or `3` or to crash.

Thus

```
*[a *[[c d] 0 *[[2 3] 0 *[a 4 4 b]]]]
```

or

```
if *[a b] then *[a c] else *[a d]
```

Converting Opcode 6 to Opcodes 0 through 5

To convert this to a single noun is straightforward enough, but it's a bit of a grind. To keep things as clean as possible, like in timluc-miptev's piece,[2] we will use variables in the dojo. Here is where we start:

```
*[a 6 b c d] == *[a *[[c d] 0 *[[2 3] 0 *[a 4 4 b]]]]
```

Let's start at the end. In order to construct `[0 *[a 4 4 b]]` on subject `a`, let's notice that it is a cell. When trying to construct a cell with respect to a subject `a` we want to put it in the form `[*[a m] *[a n]]` so that we can recover the original expression `*[a m n]`. The tail of our cell is already in the form `*[a n]`. So how about the head? `*[a 1 0] == 0`. So we can write:

```
[0 *[a 4 4 b]] == [*[a 1 0] *[a 4 4 b]] == *[a [1 0] 4 4 b]
```

Let's say `=x [[1 0] 4 4 b]`. This gives us:

```
[0 *[a 4 4 b]] == *[a x]
```

Excellent. We have started to simplify our expression. We now have:

```
*[a 6 b c d] == *[a *[[c d] 0 *[[2 3] *[a x]]]]
```

Hopefully you see how can we can repeat this process. Let's look at `*[[2 3] *[a x]]`. This has nested expression evaluations. This suggests Nock 2. For Nock 2, we want to get our expression in the form `*[*[a m] *[a n]]` so that we can recover the original expression `*[a 2 m n]`. (This looks like what we did in our first step, but don't be fooled. In the first step we were building a cell. In this step, we are building an expression evaluation.) Notice that `[2 3] == *[a 1 2 3]`. This gives us:

```
*[[2 3] *[a x]] ==
  *[*[a 1 2 3] *[a x]] ==
  *[a 2 [1 2 3] x]
```

Let's say `=y [2 [1 2 3] x]`. This gives us:

[2] See `~timluc-miptev`, pp. 1–45 in this volume.

```
*[[2 3] *[a x]] == *[a y]
```

We now have:

```
*[a 6 b c d] == *[a *[[c d] 0 *[a y]]]
```

Let's look at `[0 *[a y]]`. Another cell. We know what to do here.

```
[0 *[a y]] == [*[a 1 0] *[a y]] == *[a [1 0] y]
```

So we now have:

```
*[a 6 b c d] == *[a *[[c d] *[a [1 0] y]]]
```

`*[[c d] *[a [1 0] y]]` has nested expression evaluations. We know what to do here.

```
*[[c d] *[a [1 0] y]] ==
  *[*[a 1 c d] *[a [1 0] y]] ==
  *[a 2 [1 c d] [1 0] y]
```

This is starting to get a little verbose again. Let's substitute: `=z [2 [1 c d] [1 0] y]`. This gives us:

```
*[[c d] 0 *[[2 3] 0 *[a 4 4 b]]] ==
  *[[c d] 0 *[a y]] == *[a z]
```

So now we have:

```
*[a 6 b c d] == *[a *[a z]]
```

More nested evaluation expressions.

```
*[a *[a z]] == *[*[a 0 1] *[a z]] == *[a 2 [0 1] z]
```

Finally, we have:

```
*[a 6 b c d] == *[a 2 [0 1] z]
```

And that's the whole expression. Let's substitute back in:

```
*[a 2 [0 1] z] == *[a 2 [0 1] 2 [1 c d] [1 0] y] ==
  *[a 2 [0 1] 2 [1 c d] [1 0] 2 [1 2 3] x] ==
  *[a 2 [0 1] 2 [1 c d] [1 0] 2 [1 2 3] [1 0] 4 4 b]
```

This is Nock 6 written with only Nock 0 through 5.

Nock 6 Primitive Equivalent

```
*[a 6 b c d] ==
  *[a 2 [0 1] 2 [1 c d] [1 0] 2 [1 2 3] [1 0] 4 4 b]
```

As an aside we can notice that Nock 6 (like Nock 9) is defined as a combination of pseudocode operators and Nock opcodes. We can also go the other way to see what Nock 9 looks like in pure pseudocode operators.

```
*[a 6 b c d] ==
  *[a *[[c d] 0 *[[2 3] 0 *[a 4 4 b]]]] ==
  *[a *[[c d] 0 *[[2 3] 0 ++*[a b]]]] ==
  *[a *[[c d] 0 /[++*[a b] [2 3]]]] ==
  *[a /[/[++*[a b] [2 3]] [c d]]]
```

Nock 6 Pseudocode Operator Equivalent

```
*[a 6 b c d] == *[a /[/[++*[a b] [2 3]] [c d]]]
```

This is not quite as intuitive as the Nock 9 pseudocode operator equivalent. The definition of Nock 6 is mostly to demonstrate the very cool fact that a branching operation can be derived using only the fundamental operators * tar, / fas and + lus. But we can also look at Nock 6 another way by introducing (in our own mental fork of the Nock spec) a new pseudocode operater < gal.

Nock 6 New Pseudocode Operator

```
<[0 a b]           a
<[1 a b]           b
<a                 <a

*[a 6 b c d]       <[*[a b] *[a c] *[a d]]
```

This is equivalent to the original definition. Like # hax, this pseudocode operator is not required for Turing completeness. * tar, ? wut, + lus, = tis, and / fas are enough for this.

6 Deriving Opcode 11

Even though we don't need Nock 11 to build Nock 10, for the sake of our collective mania, let's note that Nock 11 can also trivially be written as a noun. The definition of Nock 11 is:

```
*[a 11 [b c] d] == *[[*[a c] *[a d]] 0 3]
*[a 11 b c] ====== *[a c]
```

The hint provided by this code is used in the process of jetting. In the first case, an atomic tag `b` is provided and a formula `c` is used to compute additional hint information on the subject. `d` is the formula we are actually trying to compute. In the second case, only the atomic tag `b` is passed and `c` is the formula we are actually trying to compute.

It is tempting to try to reduce the first case to `*[a d]`. However, this reduction is incorrect. You may have a case where `*[a c]` crashes but `*[a d]` does not. In this case, a correct interpreter will crash the whole expression if `*[a c]` crashes, whereas an incorrect interpreter will proceed with `*[a d]`. Thus, all correct interpreters must try to compute `*[a c]`.

```
*[a 11 [b c] d] == *[[*[a c] *[a d]] 0 3]
== *[*[a c d] *[a 1 0 3]]
== *[a 2 [c d] 1 0 3]

*[a 11 b c] == *[a c]
== *[*[a 0 1] *[a 1 c]]
== *[a 2 [0 1] 1 c]
```

Nock 11 Primitive Equivalent

```
*[a 11 [b c] d] == *[a 2 [c d] 1 0 3]
*[a 11 b c] ====== *[a 2 [0 1] 1 c]
```

Nock 11 Pseudocode Operator Equivalent

```
*[a 11 [b c] d] == /[3 [*[a c] *[a d]]]
*[a 11 b c] ====== *[a c]
```

7 Explaining Opcode 10

For convenience, let's restate Nock 10 and the # hax edit operator.

```
*[a 10 [b c] d] ==  #[b *[a c] *[a d]]

#[1 a b] ============ a
#[(a + a) b c] ====== #[a [b /[(a + a + 1) c]] c]
#[(a + a + 1) b c] == #[a [/[(a + a) c] b] c]
```

Nock 10 is defined in terms of the # hax edit operator. So let's derive this first.

7.1 The # edit operator

Let's define # hax as a function of three inputs, x, y, and z. This says replace what's in slot x of z with y. In fact, let's rewrite the pseudocode with these inputs.

```
#[(x := 1) y z] ========= y
#[(x : x is even) y z] == #[x/2 [y /[x+1 z]] z]
#[(x : x is odd) y z] === #[(x-1)/2 [/[x-1 z] y] z]
```

What are we doing here? Let's first note that there is really no way for us to "edit" a noun. Really what we are doing is producing a new noun which is exactly the same as the old noun except in the specified way. If x is 1, we are slotting into the root address of the noun z and replacing it with y, so we can get our "edited" noun simply by returning y. For any x greater than 1, however, we have to create an entirely new noun. But creating complex nouns from scratch is hard. Creating a single *cell*, on the other hand, is easy.

To make this easier to understand, let's say v := /[x z]. v is the noun we will be replacing with y; the current occupant of slot x in noun z. This noun v has a "sibling noun" which we will call w. v is either the head or the tail of its "parent noun" u. Below, we diagram the two possible cases.

```
        z                   z
       / \                 / \
      *   *               *   *
     / \                 / \
    u   *               u   *
   / \                 / \
  v   w               w   v
```

While we cannot create a modifed z in one step, we can create a modified u in one step. `u == [v w]` or `u == [w v]`. Since we are replacing v with y, our modified u looks like `u' == [y w]` in the first case and `u' == [w y]` in the second case. We already have y. We need to figure out how to get w and how to replace u. This requires the addresses of both. We diagram this below.

```
nouns          slots
-----          -----
  u             x/2
 / \            / \
v   w          x   x+1

  u           (x-1)/2
 / \            / \
w   v         x-1   x
```

If x is even, w is in slot `x+1` of z and `u' == [y /[x+1 z]]` can be slotted into slot `x/2` of z. If x is odd, w is in slot `x-1` of z and `u' == [/[x-1 z] y]` can be slotted into slot `(x-1)/2` of z. A more concise way to say this would be:

```
#[(x : x is even) y z] == #[x/2 [y /[x+1 z]] z]
#[(x : x is odd) y z] === #[(x-1)/2 [/[x-1 z] y] z]
```

This operation will recur, and since the slot is always getting smaller, we will eventually get to the base case of `x == 1` at which point we will return our new "edited" noun.

Now let's translate this into Nock. To perform this translation, we are going to make liberal use of Dojo variables to keep things relatively simple and modular.

We are trying to recreate the # hax edit operator in a function called # hax which will take a subject `[x y z]`. We should be able to run:

```
*[[x y z] hax] == #[x y z]
```

Let's crash immediately if `x` is a cell. This will make use of Nock 6. If `x-is-cell`, then `crash`; else `check-x-0` (we will proceed to check another degenerate case):

```
*[[x y z] 6 x-is-cell crash check-x-0]
```

For the sake of our OCD, we can start to convert this to opcodes 0 through 5 using our definition:

```
*[a 6 b c d] == *[a 2 [0 1]
                    2 [1 c d] [1 0] 2 [1 2 3]
                                      [1 0] 4 4 b]
```

```
=hax [2 [0 1] 2 [1 crash check-x-0]
               [1 0]
               2 [1 2 3] [1 0] 4 4 x-is-cell]
```

To check if `x` is a cell, we use Nock 3:

```
*[[x y z] 3 0 2]
=x-is-cell [3 0 2]
```

To crash, we can simply try to slot into non-existing address `0`:

```
*[[x y z] 0 0]
=crash [0 0]
```

We should also crash if `x == 0`:

```
*[[x y z] 6 x-is-0 crash launch]
=check-x-0 [2 [0 1] 2 [1 crash launch]
             [1 0] 2 [1 2 3] [1 0] 4 4 x-is-0]
```

To check if `x == 0`, we use Nock 5:

```
*[[x y z] 5 [0 2] 1 0]
=x-is-0 [5 [0 2] 1 0]
```

In order to make recursive calls, we are going to want to store our formula in the head of our subject so that we can access it from within the formula.

```
[hax-formula x y z]
```

We can do this with Nock 8 and Nock 9. With Nock 8, we will pin `hax-formula` to the head of the subject and then call this head on the modified subject using Nock 9.

```
*[[x y z] 8 [1 hax-formula] call-head]
```

Recall that `*[a 8 b c] == *[a 2 [b 0 1] 1 c]`.

```
=launch [2 [[1 hax-formula] 0 1] 1 call-head]
```

To call the head of the modified subject on itself:

```
*[[hax-formula x y z] 9 2 0 1]
```

Recall that `*[a 9 b c] == *[a 2 c 1 2 [0 1] 0 b]`.

```
*[[hax-formula x y z] 9 2 0 1] ==
  [[hax-formula x y z] 2 [0 1] 1 2 [0 1] 0 2]
```

Notice that this simplifies to:

```
=call-head [2 [0 1] 0 2]
```

Now let's develop `hax-formula`. The subject we are now dealing with has the form:

```
[hax-formula x y z]
```

- `hax-formula` is at slot 2 (the head).
- `x` is at slot 6 (the head of the tail).
- `y` is at slot 14.
- `z` is at slot 15.

Let's deal with the first real branch. If `x == 1`, then we return `y`; else, we `recur-hax`:

```
*[[hax-formula x y z] 6 x-is-1 return-y recur-hax]
=hax-formula [2 [0 1] 2 [1 return-y recur-hax]
                        [1 0]
                        2 [1 2 3] [1 0] 4 4 x-is-1]
=x-is-1 [5 [0 6] 1 1]
=return-y [0 14]
```

Excellent. Now we are getting to the recursive part of our algorithm. We have already dealt with the base case. Now in the non-base case we want to call `hax-formula` on new parameters `[new-x new-y new-z]`. Let us imagine that there is a function `new-params` which takes subject `[x y z]` and returns `[new-x new-y new-z]`. We can write this function later.

First, we want to create a cell:

```
[hax-formula new-x new-y new-z] ==
  [hax-formula *[[x y z] new-params]]

*[[hax-formula x y z] [0 2] 2 [0 3] 1 new-params]
=new-cell [[0 2] 2 [0 3] 1 new-params]
```

And we want to call the head of this new cell on itself:

```
*[[hax-formula x y z] 9 2 new-cell]
=recur-hax [2 new-cell 1 2 [0 1] 0 2]
```

When trying to extract new parameters from `[x y z]`, we come to another branch. We know at this point that `x` is not a cell and `x > 1`. Now we need to check if `x` is even:

- If `x` is even, return the following parameter updates:

  ```
  x := x/2
  y := [y /[x+1 z]]
  z := z
  ```

- Else (if `x` is odd), return the following parameter updates:

  ```
  x := (x-1)/2
  y := [/[x-1 z] y]
  z := z
  ```

So there are basically three things we need. We need a decremented `x`, `x-1`. We need a loobean which returns `0` if `x` is even and `1` otherwise (if `x` is odd; we have already dealt with all other cases). And we need the floor of half of `x`—the "parent address" of `x`.

We can actually get all of these at the same time. By using a modified version of the decrement algorithm, we can count up to `x-1` using some `counter` variable, keep track of whether `counter+1` is even or odd in variable `iseven` and keep track of the "parent address" of `counter+1` in variable `floorhalf`. When we get to `counter == x-1` we will have `x-1`, whether `x` is even, and the floor of half of `x`.

Because we are dealing with `x` values greater than `1`, the initial value of `counter` is `1`. Since the initial value of `counter+1` is `2` (the lowest possible value of `x`), the initial value of `iseven` is `0` and the initial value of `floorhalf` is `1`.

Here is what this looks like counting up to 10:

```
                        -------
                        x == 10
                        -------
+(counter)  2  3  4  5  6  7  8  9 10
counter     1  2  3  4  5  6  7  8  9
iseven      0  1  0  1  0  1  0  1  0
floorhalf   1  1  2  2  3  3  4  4  5
```

Let's look at the format of our function. Our subject is `[x y z]`. We are going to pin `[counter iseven floorhalf]` to the head of this noun and then our `params-formula` for recursion to the head of that. So by the time our recursion starts, our subject will look like this:

```
[params-formula [counter iseven floorhalf] x y z]
```

To pin `[[counter == 1] [iseven == 0] [floorhalf == 1]]` to the head of subject `[x y z]`, we run:

```
*[[x y z] 8 [1 1 0 1] pin-formula] ==
  *[[[1 0 1] x y z] pin-formula]
=new-params [2 [[1 1 0 1] 0 1] 1 pin-formula]
```

Next, we want to pin our `params-formula` to the head of this new subject:

```
*[[[1 0 1] x y z] 8 [1 params-formula] call-head] ==
  *[[params-formula [1 0 1] x y z] call-head]
=pin-formula [2 [[1 params-formula] 0 1] 1 call-head]
```

Finally, we want to run this `params-formula`, which is in the head of this new subject, against the whole subject. We actually already created a function which accomplishes this. We called it `call-head`.

```
call-head == [2 [0 1] 0 2]
```

Okay. Now we're ready to develop `params-formula`, which operates on subject:

```
[params-formula [counter iseven floorhalf] x y z]
```

(To save space we will write this as `[pf [c i f] x y z]`.)

- `params-formula` is at slot 2 (the head).
- `counter` is at slot 12 (the head of the head of the tail).
- `iseven` is at slot 26.
- `floorhalf` is at slot 27.
- `x` is at slot 14.
- `y` is at slot 30.
- `z` is at slot 31.

Our formula should check if `counter+1 == x`. If this is the case, we have all the necessary data and we can `return-params`. Else, we should increment `counter`, flip `iseven` from `0` to `1` or from `1` to `0`, increment `floorhalf` only if `iseven == 1`, and then run `params-formula` again. You should be able to convince yourself that this works.

```
*[[pf [c i f] x y z] 6 is-at-x return-params recur-pf]
=params-formula [2 [0 1] 2 [1 return-params recur-pf]
                          [1 0]
                          2 [1 2 3]
                            [1 0]
                            4 4 is-at-x]

=is-at-x [5 [0 14] 4 0 12]
```

To return parameters from `[pf [c i f] x y z]` we need to branch on `iseven`.

```
*[[pf [c i f] x y z] 6 iseven even-params odd-params]
=iseven [0 26]
=return-params [2 [0 1] 2 [1 even-params odd-params]
                         [1 0] 2 [1 2 3]
                                 [1 0] 4 4 iseven]
```

Recall that if `x` is even, return the following parameter updates:

```
x := x/2
y := [y /[x+1 z]]
z := z
```

else (if x is odd), return the following parameter updates:

```
x := (x-1)/2
y := [/[x-1 z] y]
z := z
```

This translates to the logic: If `iseven` is `0`, return:

```
[floorhalf [y /[+(x) z]] z]
```

else, return:

```
[floorhalf [/[counter z] y] z]
```

Let's try to build these cells:

```
+(x) == *[[pf [c i f] x y z] 4 0 14]
counter == *[[pf [c i f] x y z] 0 12]
z == *[[pf [c i f] x y z] 0 31]

/[+(x) z] == *[z 0 +(x)] ==
  *[*[[pf [c i f] x y z] 0 31]
    *[[pf [c i f] x y z] [1 0] 4 0 14]] ==
  *[[pf [c i f] x y z] 2 [0 31] [1 0] 4 0 14]

/[counter z] == *[z 0 counter]
== *[*[[pf [c i f] x y z] 0 31]
     *[[pf [c i f] x y z] [1 0] 0 12]]
== *[[pf [c i f] x y z] 2 [0 31] [1 0] 0 12]

[floorhalf [y /[+(x) z]] z]
== *[[pf [c i f] x y z] [0 27]
     [[0 30] 2 [0 31] [1 0] 4 0 14] 0 31]
=even-params [[0 27] [[0 30] 2 [0 31] [1 0] 4 0 14]
               0 31]

[floorhalf [/[counter z] y] z]
== *[[pf [c i f] x y z] [0 27]
     [[2 [0 31] [1 0] 0 12] 0 30] 0 31]
=odd-params [[0 27] [[2 [0 31] [1 0] 0 12] 0 30]
              0 31]
```

All right, we now have a formula to return new parameters when `x` is even and a formula to return new parameters when `x` is odd.

Now we need to actually get our modified decrement to count up to `x-1`, updating our other data with it. Remember, our `recur-pf` formula will be operating on subject:

```
[params-formula [counter iseven floorhalf] x y z]
```

We want to call `params-formula` on:

```
[params-formula [new-counter new-iseven
                 new-floorhalf] x y z]
```

We can do this by calling:

```
*[[pf [c i f] x y z] 9 2 [0 2]
  [new-counter new-iseven new-floorhalf] 0 7]
```

`[[0 2] [new-counter new-iseven new-floorhalf 0 7]]` creates the new subject as a cell and the opcode 9 launches the head 2 on this new subject.

```
=recur-pf [2 [[0 2]
              [new-counter new-iseven new-floorhalf]
              0 7]] 1 2 [0 1] 0 2]
```

Now let's actually update these values. `new-counter` is easy enough. It just increments the existing counter.

```
=new-counter [4 0 12]
```

`new-iseven` checks `iseven` then returns `1` if yes or `0` if no.

```
*[[pf [c i f] x y z] 6 iseven [1 1] 1 0]
=new-iseven [2 [0 1] 2 [1 [1 1] 1 0] [1 0]
            2 [1 2 3] [1 0] 4 4 iseven]
```

`new-floorhalf` checks `iseven` and returns `floorhalf` if yes or `+(floorhalf)` if no.

```
*[[pf [c i f] x y z] 6 iseven [0 27] 4 0 27]
=new-floorhalf [2 [0 1] 2 [1 [0 27] 4 0 27] [1 0]
               2 [1 2 3] [1 0] 4 4 iseven]
```

Okay! We have written our # hax edit operator as a Nock formula consisting of only Nocks 0 through 5. Very exciting! Let's put it together and see what it looks like. If you would like to try this yourself, copy and paste the following code in the dojo.

```
=iseven [0 26]
=new-counter [4 0 12]
=new-iseven [2 [0 1] 2 [1 [1 1] 1 0] [1 0]
             2 [1 2 3] [1 0] 4 4 iseven]
=new-floorhalf [2 [0 1] 2 [1 [0 27] 4 0 27] [1 0]
                2 [1 2 3] [1 0] 4 4 iseven]
=recur-pf [2 [[0 2]
              [new-counter new-iseven new-floorhalf]
              0 7] 1 2 [0 1] 0 2]
=odd-params [[0 27] [[2 [0 31] [1 0] 0 12] 0 30]
             0 31]
=even-params [[0 27] [[0 30] 2 [0 31] [1 0] 4 0 14]
              0 31]
=return-params [2 [0 1] 2 [1 even-params odd-params]
                [1 0] 2 [1 2 3] [1 0] 4 4 iseven]
=is-at-x [5 [0 14] 4 0 12]
=params-formula [2 [0 1] 2 [1 return-params recur-pf]
                 [1 0] 2 [1 2 3] [1 0] 4 4 is-at-x]
=call-head [2 [0 1] 0 2]
=pin-formula [2 [[1 params-formula] 0 1] 1 call-head]
=new-params [2 [[1 1 0 1] 0 1] 1 pin-formula]
=new-cell [[0 2] 2 [0 3] 1 new-params]
=recur-hax [2 new-cell 1 2 [0 1] 0 2]
=x-is-1 [5 [0 6] 1 1]
=return-y [0 14]
=hax-formula [2 [0 1] 2 [1 return-y recur-hax]
              [1 0] 2 [1 2 3] [1 0] 4 4 x-is-1]
=launch [2 [[1 hax-formula] 0 1] 1 call-head]
=x-is-0 [5 [0 2] 1 0]
=crash [0 0]
=check-x-0 [2 [0 1] 2 [1 crash launch] [1 0]
            2 [1 2 3] [1 0] 4 4 x-is-0]
=x-is-cell [3 0 2]

=hax [2 [0 1] 2 [1 crash check-x-0] [1 0] 2 [1 2 3]
      [1 0] 4 4 x-is-cell]
```

Great! What does this look like?

```
::  hax definition in raw Nock
[2 [0 1]
   2 [1 [0 0]
      2 [0 1]
        2 [1 [0 0]
           2 [[1 2 [0 1]
                   2 [1 [0 14]
                      2 [[0 2]
                         2 [0 3]
                         1 2 [[1 1 0 1] 0 1]
                             1 2 [[1 2 [0 1]
                                   2 [1 [2 [0 1]
                                           2 [1
  ↳ [[0 27] [[0 30] 2 [0 31] [1 0] 4 0 14] 0 31]
   [0 27]
   [[2 [0 31] [1 0] 0 12] 0 30]
                                              0 31]
                                             [1 0]
                                           2 [1 2 3]
                                             [1 0]
                                             4 4 0 26]
                                      2 [[0 2]
                                         [[4 0 12]
  ↳ [2 [0 1]
       2 [1 [1 1] 1 0]
         [1 0]
         2 [1 2 3]
           [1 0]
           4 4 0 26]
    2 [0 1]
      2 [1 [0 27] 4 0 27]
        [1 0]
        2 [1 2 3]
          [1 0]
          4 4 0 26]
                                         0 7]
                                      1 2 [0 1]
                                      0 2]
                                     [1 0]
                                     2 [1 2 3]
                                       [1 0]
```

```
                                     4 4 5 [0 14]
                                 4 0 12]
                                0 1]
                         1 2 [0 1]
                       0 2]
                      1 2 [0 1]
                     0 2]
                  [1 0]
          2 [1 2 3]
            [1 0]
            4 4 5 [0 6]
              1 1]
          0 1]
        1 2 [0 1]
      0 2]
    [1 0]
    2 [1 2 3]
      [1 0]
    4 4 5 [0 2]
    1 0]
[1 0]
2 [1 2 3]
  [1 0]
  4 4 3 0 2]
```

Quite a mouthful. I don't think this one will fit on a t-shirt. Maybe an evening gown, or perhaps a toga.

So, does it work?

```
> .*([1 [4 5] 6 7 8 9 10 11 12 13] hax)
[4 5]

> .*([2 [4 5] 6 7 8 9 10 11 12 13] hax)
[[4 5] 7 8 9 10 11 12 13]

> .*([3 [4 5] 6 7 8 9 10 11 12 13] hax)
[6 4 5]

> .*([62 [4 5] 6 7 8 9 10 11 12 13] hax)
[6 7 8 9 [4 5] 11 12 13]

> .*([17 [4 5] [[[[[[[6] 7] 8] 9] 10] 11] 12] 13]
    hax)
```

```
[[[[[[[6 7] 8] 9] 4 5] 11] 12] 13]
```

It appears so! We are inches away from the finish line.

8 Deriving Opcode 10

We now have our # hax operator. The last thing we have to do is use it to create a Nock 10 which runs on subject `a` with parameters `b`, `c`, and `d`:

```
*[a 10 [b c] d] == #[b *[a c] *[a d]]
```

Recall that we wrote # hax such that:

```
*[[x y z] hax] == #[x y z]
```

We can now rewrite this as:

```
*[a 10 [b c] d] ==
  *[[b *[a c] *[a d]] hax] ==
  *[[*[a 1 b] *[a c d]] *[a 1 hax]] ==
  *[*[a [1 b] c d] *[a 1 hax]] ==
  *[a 2 [[1 b] c d] 1 hax]
=nock-ten [2 [[1 b] c d] 1 hax]
```

And that's it. Congratulations! You have now derived all the Nock opcodes from 6 to 11 using only opcodes 0 through 5. What you will accomplish with this knowledge, I tremble to imagine. ⌘

Nock 10 Primitive Equivalent

```
*[a 10 [b c] d] ==
*[a 2 [[1 b] c d]
      1 2 [0 1]
          2 [1 [0 0]
             2 [0 1]
               2 [1 [0 0]
                  2 [[1 2 [0 1]
                      2 [1 [0 14]
                         2 [[0 2]
                            2 [0 3]
                        1 2 [[1 1 0 1] 0 1]
                        1 2 [[1 2 [0 1]
 ↳  2 [1 [2 [0 1]
          2 [1 [[0 27]
                [[0 30]
                  2 [0 31]
                    [1 0]
                    4 0 14]
                0 31]
                [0 27]
                [[2 [0 31]
                    [1 0]
                    0 12]
                  0 30]
              0 31]
              [1 0]
              2 [1 2 3]
                [1 0]
                4 4 0 26]
          2 [[0 2]
             [[4 0 12]
              [2 [0 1]
                  2 [1 [1 1] 1 0]
                    [1 0]
                    2 [1 2 3]
                      [1 0]
                      4 4 0 26]
              2 [0 1]
              2 [1 [0 27] 4 0 27]
                [1 0]
```

```
              2 [1 2 3]
                [1 0]
                4 4 0 26]
            0 7]
     1 2 [0 1] 0 2]
     [1 0]
     2 [1 2 3]
       [1 0]
       4 4 5 [0 14] 4 0 12]
                            0 1]
                        1 2 [0 1] 0 2]
             1 2 [0 1] 0 2]
        [1 0]
        2 [1 2 3]
          [1 0]
          4 4 5 [0 6]
        1 1]
      0 1]
    1 2 [0 1] 0 2]
  [1 0]
  2 [1 2 3]
    [1 0]
    4 4 5 [0 2] 1 0]
[1 0]
2 [1 2 3]
  [1 0]
  4 4 3 0 2]
```

Metacircular Virtualization & Practical Nock Interpretation

~lacnes

Abstract

This paper presents a detailed examination of metacircular virtualization in the Nock combinator calculus, focusing on the practical implementation of a virtualized Nock interpreter within the Urbit ecosystem. We explore the design and functionality of key components, including the `++mink` interpreter, and their roles in enabling robust Nock execution environments. Extensions of Nock using fake opcodes, particularly opcode 12, are discussed, and a minimal working example of a Nock-virtualized Nock formula is provided.

Contents

Urbit Systems Technical Journal II:2 (2025): 71–97.
Address author correspondence to ~lacnes.

1 Introduction

The Nock combinator calculus is used as a target instruction set architecture (ISA) for the Hoon and Jock languages. However, Nock itself is a "crash-only" paradigm which has no error handling mechanism within the terms of the ISA itself. Furthermore, sometimes information is necessary to complete a calculation which may not be present in the apparent subject. Practical Nock interpreters handle this by running Nock within Nock, a process of metacircular virtualization. This article explores the design of `++mock`, the basic virtualized Nock interpreter, and its role within a Nock-based kernel and standard library.

2 Background

In 1958, John McCarthy began his lifelong work on the Lisp programming language (McCarthy, 1996). While the form would evolve over the years, the fundamental components included S-expressions, or parenthesized lists of homoiconic code–data;

' or quote, a deferred expression; and `eval`, a function to evaluate quoted code.[1] Together these components allowed McCarthy and colleague Steve Russell to implement a Lisp interpreter in Lisp itself, the first metacircular interpreter (McCarthy and Wexelblat, 1978). Such was a radical departure from the imperative programming paradigm of the time, exemplified in Fortran (1954–55); Lisp's reliance on recursion and higher-order functions was both a precursor to the functional program paradigm and a rejuvenation of the Church and Curry schools of fundamental computing logic.

Metacircularity was considered sufficiently important that several programming languages implemented it as a first-class feature, including Forth, TeX, and Prolog. They have generally been used either for tightly interpreted features like debuggers and code introspection tools, or for language extensions like macros.

Amin and Rompf (2017) analyzed how metacircular interpreters build on top of each other, each adding a new layer of abstraction. While primarily considering a Lisp dialect, they showed how interpreted language extensions (even in cascading towers) can be collapsed to bottom-level interpretation, similar to Nock's own `++mink` function. They epitomized a line of research on reflective languages and self-interpreted languages, such as quasiquotation in Lisp (Bawden, 1999) and Template Meta-Haskell (Sheard and Jones, 2002). The ultimate point of this enquiry was to show that metacircularity was a powerful and well-grounded tool for building interpreters, and that it could be used to in fact build practical interpreters.

Before Nock was even christened, one of its earliest design criteria was to straightforwardly implement a metacircular interpreter (`~sorreg-namtyv`, 2006; `~sorreg-namtyv`, 2010). While the original motivation was to implement a hyper-Turing operator over a referentially transparent bound namespace, Nock's support for virtualization also soon proved useful for managing error traces and crashes. Yarvin wrote in an early document:

[1] Paul Graham, in his 2001 short essay "What Made Lisp Different", grouped these concepts into the phrase "The whole language always available" (2001).

> Metacircularity in most languages is a curiosity and corner case. Programmers are routinely warned not to use it, and for good reason. Practical metacircularity is a particular strength of Nock, or any functional assembly language. Dynamic loading and/or virtualization works, at least logically, as in an OS.
>
> We hypothesize that a metacircular functional dissemination protocol can serve as a complete, general-purpose system software environment—there is no problem it cannot solve, in theory or in practice. Such a protocol can be described as an "operating function" or *OF*—the functional analog of an imperative operating system. (`~sorreg-namtyv`, 2010)

Metacircularity thus closely ties to the idea of a functional operating system. This is a theme that has been explored in other contexts, such as the Lisp machines and the Haskell GHC runtime system. For Nock, a virtualized interpreter is no mere corner case but a first-class component of the system, both for practical execution and for resource discovery.

3 Virtualized Nock

Given an argument for metacircularity, we can now examine how Nock is actually virtualized in practice. The Urbit standard library provides a metacircular Nock interpreter, `++mink`, along with several other components for building virtualized Nock environments. Some essential components provided by vanilla Hoon for virtualizing Nock include:

- `++mink`, compute bottom-level virtual Nock.
- `++mock`, compute formula on subject with hint. Wraps `++mink`; common entrypoint.
- `++mule`, kick a trap (deferred computation). Wraps `++mock`; common entrypoint.

- `++soft`, wrap a typecast as a unit (i.e., fail with `~` rather than crash).

Nock execution environments virtualize Nock for two primary reasons:

1. Crash handling (provisional execution).
2. Language extension (additional opcodes).

3.1 Crash handling

While virtualization necessarily incurs some overhead relative to more direct execution, it gives the Nock programmer a way to bail (crash), trace (log with debugging information), and bind (time-limit) a computation. In fact, stack traces are computed through virtualization, and so are guaranteed to be as correct as their implementation.

A Nock virtualization environment needs to distinguish at least three kinds of results:

1. A successful result of computation, along with a valid Nock noun.
2. A block, which indicates that the computation is not yet complete and should be continued.
3. A halt or deterministic error, which indicates that the computation has failed and should not be continued.

These correspond to standard scry results (see "Opcode 12" below) in this order:

1. `[~ ~ noun]`, a successful result.
2. `~`, a result is not currently available (block).
3. `[~ ~]`, a result will never become available (halt).

Because Nock is untyped and we need to distinguish a "zero" from a "block", the structure of each scry result fundamentally differs from the other options.

Nondeterministic errors—crashes in the runtime, such as an out-of-memory error—are not handled by or visible to the Nock interpreter as a solid-state computer.

3.2 Language extension

Virtualization enables the extension of Nock using "fake opcodes". At the current time, only opcode 12 has been added;[2] this opcode provides a generalized way to supply the OS context to the scope in a way that appears like a `GOTO` or remote call but actually preserves Nock semantics including strict subject scoping. There is a sense in which the scry operation and the bound (referentially transparent) scry namespace are identical to the metacircularity of the Nock interpreter itself. The operating function itself can be treated as a first-class member of its own ecosystem.

Hoon defines `+$nock` already suited for virtualized Nock execution including fake opcode 12 (Listing 1).

However, while `++mink` is compiled to and evaluated in Nock, it is written in Hoon and accordingly uses Hoon's affordances, particularly vases. Vases are a pair of type and data intended to store relevant type information for correctly evaluating raw untyped Nock nouns.[3] Accordingly, it is Hoon's higher-level introspective tools that facilitate `++mink`'s operation.

The remainder of this section analyzes how each `++mink` implements each Nock opcode, including particularly the fake opcode 12. The following code samples are taken from `/sys/hoon` in the Urbit codebase.

`++mink` produces a head atom marking the kind of result the interpreter has raised: if a `%0`, the result is a valid Nock noun; if a `%1`, a block is indicated (i.e. the halting problem continues); if a `%2`, then a deterministic error has occurred with an error trace.

3.3 Opcode 0

Opcode 0 is the identity function, which returns its argument unchanged. This is implemented in `++mink` as follows:

---

[2]Compare, however, the approach of `~barpub-tarber`, pp. 191–228 in this volume, who presented an explicitly constructive Nock-like paradigm in Ax.

[3]See `~lagrev-nocfep`, pp. 131–153 in this volume, for a discussion of vases and their role in practical Nock compilation.

Listing 1: Hoon's +$nock specification

```
::              ::::::  virtual nock
+$  nock   $^  ::  autocons
               [p=nock q=nock]
           $%  ::  constant
               [%1 p=*]
               ::  compose
               [%2 p=nock q=nock]
               ::  cell test
               [%3 p=nock]
               ::  increment
               [%4 p=nock]
               ::  equality test
               [%5 p=nock q=nock]
               ::  if, then, else
               [%6 p=nock q=nock r=nock]
               ::  serial compose
               [%7 p=nock q=nock]
               ::  push onto subject
               [%8 p=nock q=nock]
               ::  select arm and fire
               [%9 p=@ q=nock]
               ::  edit
               [%10 p=[p=@ q=nock] q=nock]
               ::  hint
               [%11 p=$@(@ [p=@ q=nock]) q=nock]
               ::  grab data from sky
               [%12 p=nock q=nock]
               ::  axis select
               [%0 p=@]
           ==
```

```
:: *[a 0 b]      /[b a]
  [%0 axis=@]
=/  part  (frag axis.formula subject)
?~  part  [%2 trace]
[%0 u.part]
```

In essence, an axis is provisionally extracted from the subject; if this is ~ then an error is raised with the current execution trace, else the resulting value from that axis is produced.

3.4 Opcode 1

Opcode 1 is the constant function, which returns a constant value extricated from the formula. This is implemented in `++mink` as follows:

```
:: *[a 1 b]      b
  [%1 constant=*]
[%0 constant.formula]
```

3.5 Opcode 2

Opcode 2 is the evaluation function, which evaluates the formula on the subject. This is implemented in `++mink` as follows:

```
:: *[a 2 b c]    *[*[a b] *[a c]]
  [%2 subject=* formula=*]
=/  subject  $(formula subject.formula)
?.  ?=(%0 -.subject)  subject
=/  formula  $(formula formula.formula)
?.  ?=(%0 -.formula)  formula
%=  $
  subject  product.subject
  formula  product.formula
==
```

Errors are passed directly through, whereas the resulting formula is invoked on the resulting subject.

3.6 Opcode 3

Opcode 3 is the cell test function, which tests whether the subject is a cell. This is implemented in `++mink` as follows:

```
::  *[a 3 b]        ?*[a b]
  [%3 subject=*]
=/  argument  $(formula argument.formula)
?.  ?=(%0 -.argument)  argument
[%0 .?(product.argument)]
```

This reduces to an evaluation of a base-level opcode 3 after a preliminary check that the formula evaluates correctly.

3.7 Opcode 4

Opcode 4 is the increment function, which increments the subject. This is implemented in `++mink` as follows:

```
::  *[a 4 b]        +*[a b]
  [%4 subject=*]
=/  argument  $(formula argument.formula)
?.  ?=(%0 -.argument)  argument
?^  product.argument  [%2 trace]
[%0 .+(product.argument)]
```

Note that like opcode 3, this reduces to an evaluation of a base-level opcode 4.

3.8 Opcode 5

Opcode 5 is the equality test function, which tests whether the subject and formula are equal. This is implemented in `++mink` as follows:

```
::  *[a 5 b c]      =[*[a b] *[a c]]
  [%5 subject=* formula=*]
=/  a  $(formula a.formula)
?.  ?=(%0 -.a)  a
=/  b  $(formula b.formula)
?.  ?=(%0 -.b)  b
[%0 =(product.a product.b)]
```

Like opcodes 3 and 4, this reduces to an evaluation of a base-level opcode 5 after checking the left-hand and right-hand formulas.

3.9 Opcode 6

Opcode 6 is the if-then-else or conditional branch function, which evaluates the formula on the subject and then evaluates either the first or second formula depending on the result. This is implemented in `++mink` as follows:

```
::  *[a 6 b c d]   *[a *[[c d] 0 *[[2 3] 0 *[a 4 4 b]]]]
  [%6 test=* yes=* no=*]
=/  result  $(formula test.formula)
?.  ?=(%0 -.result)  result
?+  product.result
      [%2 trace]
  %&  $(formula yes.formula)
  %|  $(formula no.formula)
==
```

As with the direct opcode 6, there is no short-circuit evaluation in the conditional statement.

3.10 Opcode 7

Opcode 7 is the composition function, which evaluates the formula on the subject and then evaluates the next formula on the result. This is implemented in `++mink` as follows:

```
::  *[a 7 b c]          *[*[a b] c]
  [%7 subject=* next=*]
=/  subject  $(formula subject.formula)
?.  ?=(%0 -.subject)  subject
%=  $
  subject  product.subject
  formula  next.formula
==
```

This implementation simply drops the evaluation of `subject` through as the explicit subject for the next formula.

3.11 Opcode 8

Opcode 8 is the variable push function, which pushes a value onto the subject. This is implemented in `++mink` as follows:

```
:: *[a 8 b c]                 *[[*[a b] a] c]
  [%8 head=* next=*]
=/  head  $(formula head.formula)
?.  ?=(%0 -.head)  head
%=  $
  subject  [product.head subject]
  formula  next.formula
==
```

Here the conceptual differences between opcode 7 and opcode 8 can be sharply compared: how 7 requires an evaluation against the current subject, leading to something of the nature of $c(b(a))$ in terms of function composition, versus how 8 simply augments the subject.

3.12 Opcode 9

Opcode 9 is the arm select function, which selects an arm of the subject and evaluates it. This is implemented in `++mink` as follows:

```
:: *[a 9 b c]     *[*[a c] 2 [0 1] 0 b]
  [%9 axis=@ core=*]
=/  core  $(formula core.formula)
?.  ?=(%0 -.core)  core
=/  arm  (frag axis.formula product.core)
?~  arm  [%2 trace]
%=  $
  subject  product.core
  formula  u.arm
==
```

For all the mechanics involved in opcode 9, the implementation is perhaps surprisingly simple. Extract the arm at the axis and evaluate it structurally using an opcode 2. (As an aside, Hoon which compiles to Nock aggressively utilizes lambdas to define functions at the point of use, and frequently employs a gate-building gate pattern. This latter resolves to two opcodes 9 in series.)

3.13 Opcode 10

Opcode 10 is the edit function, which edits a value in the subject at the given axis. This is implemented in `++mink` as follows:

```
::  *[a 10 [b c] d]  #[b *[a c] *[a d]]
  [%10 [axis=@ value=*] target=*]
?:  =(0 axis.formula)  [%2 trace]
=/  target  $(formula target.formula)
?.  ?=(%0 -.target)  target
=/  value  $(formula value.formula)
?.  ?=(%0 -.value)  value
=/  mutant=(unit *)
  (edit axis.formula product.target product.value)
?~  mutant  [%2 trace]
[%0 u.mutant]
```

`++edit` traverses the noun to attempt to access a given axis; if it succeeds, it returns a new noun with the original value at that axis replaced by a new target value. If it fails, it returns an empty `unit`, indicating without a crash that the edit failed.

There's more plumbing here because of the mutation of the noun, but the essential concept of locating and replacing a valid subtree is straightforward.

3.14 Opcode 11

Opcode 11 is the hint function, which provides a hint to the interpreter about how to interpret the argument. This is the only way to produce side effects from Nock as a pure function, and `++mink` respects and passes through hints raised by the virtualized Nock formula. This is implemented in `++mink` as follows:

```
::  *[a 11 b c]        *[a c]
::  *[a 11 [b c] d]    *[[*[a c] *[a d]] 0 3]
  [%11 tag=@ next=*]
```

```
=/  next  $(formula next.formula)
?.  ?=(%0 -.next)  next
:-  %0
.*  subject
[11 tag.formula 1 product.next]
::
  [%11 [tag=@ clue=*] next=*]
=/  clue  $(formula clue.formula)
?.  ?=(%0 -.clue)  clue
=/  next
  =?    trace
      ?=(?(%hunk %hand %lose %mean %spot) tag.formula)
    [[tag.formula product.clue] trace]
  $(formula next.formula)
?.  ?=(%0 -.next)  next
:-  %0
.*  subject
[11 [tag.formula 1 product.clue] 1 product.next]
```

Two options match for opcode 11, a static and a dynamic hint. Even though this virtualized code "sandboxes" execution, the Nock formula including the `clue` is in fact evaluated. The runtime listens for a `clue`, which is compared to a whitelisted set of supported hints, as in normal (nonvirtualized) Nock execution.

Note that the argument cannot simply be discarded by the interpreter, because it may result in a crash. Thus, as with direct Nock execution, the hint must be evaluated.[4]

[4]Here, this should be read "evaluated safely", with the caveat that some hints may result in a runtime crash. For instance, an ill-formed `%slog` hint (`printf`) will crash the interpreter if the `clue` is not structured correctly. This is a consequence of the fact that Nock is untyped and so the interpreter cannot know whether the hint is well-formed or not. The `++mink` interpreter does not attempt to validate hints, but merely passes them through to the runtime for evaluation. (One could imagine a Nock virtualizer which itself handled certain hints as if they were "side effects" to the evaluation.)

3.15 Opcode 12

Opcode 12 is the scry function, which retrieves a value from the `sky` namespace environment.[5] This is implemented in `++mink` as follows:

```
  [%12 ref=* path=*]
=/  ref  $(formula ref.formula)
?.  ?=(%0 -.ref)  ref
=/  path  $(formula path.formula)
?.  ?=(%0 -.path)  path
=/  result  (scry product.ref product.path)
?~  result
  [%1 product.path]
?~  u.result
  [%2 [%hunk product.ref product.path] trace]
[%0 u.u.result]
```

Opcode 12 does not have a direct Nock expression since it "steps outside" the subject–formula pair via the expedient of the `scry` gate.

> In order to interpret opcode 12, `++mink` takes as an argument, in addition to the subject and formula, a gate which will be invoked with the results of the subformulas of 12 as a sample. The result of executing this gate (not as interpreted by `++mink` but by whichever interpreter is running `++mink`) are then treated as the result of the Nock 12 operation. ("4n `++mink`", Urbit documentation)

Much of consequence is entailed by the use of a `scry` gate, which is a Hoon function that retrieves a value from an associated `sky` namespace (nominally, the bound scry namespace, although this is not necessarily entailed by Urbit in contemporary practice). The `scry` function bears the signature `$-(^ (unit (unit)))`

[5] There is a sense in which opcodes 6–11 are also virtualized extensions to Nock, acting as they do as macros. See `~niblyx-malnus`, pp. 47–70 in this volume.

The result of this operation is either a noun or a block, and it is returned as a `(unit (unit noun))`. These correspond to standard scry results in this order:

1. `[~ ~ noun]`, a successful result.
2. `~`, a result is not currently available (block).
3. `[~ ~]`, a result will never become available (halt).

For instance, the reference `roof` function for Arvo, the Urbit kernel, is schematically defined as:

```
++  roof
  |$  [vase]
  $-  $:  lyc=(unit (set ship))       ::  leakset
          pov=path                    ::  provenance
          [vis=view bem=beam]         ::  perspective
      ==                              ::
  %-  unit                            ::  ~          unknown
  %-  unit                            ::  ~ ~        invalid
  (pair mark vase)                    ::  envased result
+$  view  $@(term [way=term car=term]) ::  perspective
```

An excursus is here warranted. The Arvo core is the Nock-based kernel of Urbit, and it is responsible for managing the state of the system and providing a consistent interface for agents to interact with that state. The Arvo core is built on top of the Nock interpreter, and it uses the `++mink` function to interpret Nock formulas. Each vane in the Arvo core receives a `+$roof` in its function call, which it can call when it needs to scry with opcode 12. This gate provides access to the vane's state, and it is used to retrieve values from the vane's state in a way that is consistent with the Nock semantics.

`++look` is a gate that is used to convert the `++mink`-compatible version of the scry handler into a version that can be used by the Arvo core. This gate acts as a bridge between the `.^` dotket and the scry handler (`++look`) with access to the roof that came from the vane. This pattern imposes constraints on interpreters, but provides a way to mediate access to the state of the system in a way that is consistent with Nock semantics.

Thus `.^` dotket gives mediated access into the `sky` without exposing the state of the entire system in the subject (untyped permissions-free access).

3.16 Et cetera

`++mink` also features some machinery to correctly implement the cell distribution rule.

```
  [^ *]
=/  head  $(formula -.formula)
?.  ?=(%0 -.head)  head
=/  tail  $(formula +.formula)
?.  ?=(%0 -.tail)  tail
[%0 product.head product.tail]
```

`++mink` is naturally jetted for efficiency, ultimately by `u3m_soft_run()` in Urbit's Vere (C) and by `interpret()` in NockApp's NockVM (formerly Sword) (Rust), both the virtualization context for their respective runtimes. Some internal affordances for the runtime are in place to keep execution consistent; e.g., scry gates are stored on a stack to prevent re-entry if it scries.

Nock is a crash-only language, which means that when something goes wrong, the exception is an exception for the runtime or virtual machine to handle as it will. Typically, for a runtime this means an injection of the error trace back into the Nock kernel (cf. section "`u3n`: nock execution" in `u3.md` in the Urbit documentation[6]). (For `++mink`, errors are attempted to be front-run by the interpreter and thus bad Nock should not be executed as such.)

4 Nock in Nock

Hearkening back to Amin and Rompf's collapsed towers of interpreters, the affordances of `++mock` as a metacircular interpreter permit us to build a tower of interpreters on top of it

[6] This section devoted a fair amount of attention to opcode 11 now 12 (it being written for Nock 5K) and hint evaluation.

without incurring excessive performance overhead. As the author of `u3.md` concluded for the Vere C runtime, "we simply treat Nock proper as a special case of `mock`." The conventional `++mink` gate is built in Hoon, but what if we stripped it down and built it in Nock itself with the minimal necessary machinery? What would such an interpreter look like, and how would it relate to actual operation on a runtime in practice?

Let us extend `++mink` to implement a logical loobean operator. (Call the modified gate `++pink`.) This operation will be invoked with a new fake opcode 13. Under the hood, opcode 13 will simply logically negate a value (via an opcode 6).

```
::  *[a 13 b]                        NOT *[a b]
  [%13 subject=*]
=/  argument  $(formula argument.formula)
?.  ?=(%0 -.argument)  [%2 trace]
?^  product.argument  [%2 trace]
?:  =(%1 product.argument)  [%0 %.y]
?:  =(%0 product.argument)  [%0 %.n]
[%2 trace]
```

This is invoked as:

```
> (pink [0 13 1 0] *$-(^ (unit (unit))))
[%0 product=0]
> (pink [0 13 1 1] *$-(^ (unit (unit))))
[%0 product=1]
> (pink [0 13 1 2] *$-(^ (unit (unit))))
[%2 trace=~]
```

Finally, it is instructive to consider what the minimal required amount of code machinery would be for one to successfully implement a Nock metacircular interpreter in Nock itself. An examination of `++mink` shows modest reliance on Hoon's higher-level features; tree math, for instance, in `++cap` for distinguishing head vs. tail and `++mas` for finding the relative address of an axis. (Neither of these are particularly complicated, but they entail some basic arithmetic operations as well.) By omitting `++scry` and opcode 12, as well as reducing to a structural match with a `+$tone` instead of an explicit Hoon type match, one could produce a reasonably sized Hoon program compiling to something close to the minimal viable Nock virtualized interpreter. No doubt intrepid code golfers will find it very much an upper bound rather than a lower.

This Nock formula produces a working virtualized Nock interpreter derived from Hoon code with some hand tuning. The input function signature is `[subject=* formula=*]` with output of the form `[@ product=*]`; if the head is `%0`, then the product is a valid Nock noun, while a head of `%bail` indicates a crash in the evaluation. Opcode 9 calls may be addressed into the core as subject, and the formula itself is complete with an empty subject.

```
[[1
  [:: +mul multiplication of two atoms
   8 [1 1 1]
     [1 8 [1 0]
        8 [1 6 [5 [1 0] 0 60]
               [0 6]
               9 2 10 [60 8 [9 686 0 31]
                             9 2 10 [6 0 124] 0 2]
                   10 [6 8 [9 20 0 31]
                             9 2 10 [6 [0 125] 0 14]
                       0 2] 0 1]
      9 2 0 1] 0 1]
  [[:: +add addition of two atoms
    8 [1 0 0]
      [1 6 [5 [1 0] 0 12]
           [0 13]
           9 2 10
           [6 [8 [9 686 0 7] 9 2 10 [6 0 28] 0 2]
            4 0 13]
         0 1] 0 1]
     [[8
       :: +list type definition
        [8 [1 0]
           [1 8 [0 6] 8 [5 [0 14] 0 2] 0 6]
         0 1]
        [1 8 [1 0]
          [1 8
              [6 [3 0 6]
                 [[6 [5 [1 0] 0 12] [1 0] 0 0]
                 8 [0 30] 9 2 10 [6 0 29] 0 2]
```

```
        6 [5 [1 0] 0 6] [1 0] 0 0]
      8 [5 [0 14] 0 2] 0 6]
    0 1] 0 1]
[:: +dvr division with remainder
 8 [1 1 1]
   [1 6 [5 [1 0] 0 13]
        [0 0]
        8 [1 0]
        8 [1 6 [8 [9 687 0 31]
                9 2 10 [6 [0 124] 0 125] 0 2]
           [[0 6] 0 60]
           9 2 10
           [60 8 [9 23 0 31]
                 9 2 10 [6 [0 124] 0 125] 0 2]
           10 [6 4 0 6] 0 1]
     9 2 0 1] 0 1]
 [:: +cap:
  8 [1 0]
    [1 6 [5 [1 2] 0 6]
         [1 2]
         6 [5 [1 3] 0 6]
           [1 3]
           6 [6 [5 [1 1] 0 6] [1 0] 5 [1 0] 0 6]
             [0 0]
             9 2 10
             [6 7 [8 [9 170 0 7]
                      9 2 10
                      [6 [0 14] 7 [0 3] 1 2]
                   0 2] 0 2]
     0 1] 0 1]
 [:: +dec decrement an atom
  8 [1 0]
    [1 6 [5 [1 0] 0 6]
         [0 0]
         8 [1 0]
         8 [1 6 [5 [0 30] 4 0 6]
                [0 6]
                9 2 10 [6 4 0 6] 0 1]
     9 2 0 1] 0 1]
 :: +lth less-than test
 8 [1 0 0]
   [1 6 [6 [5 [0 12] 0 13] [1 1] 1 0]
```

```
         [6 [8
             [1 6 [5 [1 0] 0 28]
                  [1 0]
                  6 [6 [6 [5 [1 0] 0 29]
                          [1 1]
                          1 0]
                       [6 [9 2 10
                           [14 [8 [9 686 0 15]
                                9 2 10 [6 0 60]
                                0 2]
                            8 [9 686 0 15]
                            9 2 10 [6 0 61] 0 2]
                           0 1]
                          [1 0]
                          1 1]
                      1 1]
               [1 0] 1 1] 9 2 0 1]
      [1 0] 1 1] 1 1] 0 1]
[:: +edit edit an atom at a given axis
 8 [1 0 0 0]
   [1 6 [5 [1 1] 0 12]
        [[1 0] 0 27]
        6 [6 [3 0 26] [1 1] 1 0]
          [1 0]
          8 [9 2 10 [26
                     8 [8 [9 342 0 63]
                          9 2 10 [6 0 28] 0 2]
                     6 [5 [1 2] 0 2]
                       [0 116]
                       6 [5 [1 3] 0 2]
                         [0 117]
                         1 1.818.845.538 0]
                       10 [12 8 [9 87 0 63]
                           9 2 10 [6 0 28] 0 2]
              0 1]
            6 [5 [1 0] 0 2]
              [1 0]
              8 [8 [9 342 0 15]
                   9 2 10 [6 0 60] 0 2]
                6 [5 [1 2] 0 2]
                  [7 [0 3] [1 0] [0 5] 0 117]
                  6 [5 [1 3] 0 2]
```

```
                  [7 [0 3] [1 0] [0 116] 0 5]
                  1 1.818.845.538 0]
 0 1]
[:: +jink, raw virtual Nock
 8 [1 0 0]
   [1 8
      6  :: Cell distribution
      [6 [3 0 13] [3 0 26] 1 1]
      [8 [9 2 10 [13 0 26] 0 1]
        6 [5 [1 0] 0 4]
          [8 [9 2 10 [13 0 59] 0 3]
            6 [5 [1 0] 0 4]
              [[1 0] [0 13] 0 5]
           0 2]
       0 2]
      6  :: Opcode 0
      [6 [3 0 13]
         [6 [5 [1 0] 0 26]
            [6 [3 0 27] [1 1] 1 0]
            1 1]
         1 1]
      [8 [8 [9 22 0 7]
            9 2 10 [6 [0 59] 0 28] 0 2]
         6 [5 [1 0] 0 2]
           [1 1.818.845.538 0]
           [1 0]
         0 5]
      6  :: Opcode 1
      [6 [3 0 13]
         [5 [1 1] 0 26] 1 1]
      [[1 0] 0 27]
      6  :: Opcode 2
      [6 [3 0 13]
         [6 [5 [1 2] 0 26] [3 0 27] 1 1] 1 1]
      [8 [9 2 10 [13 0 54] 0 1]
         6 [5 [1 0] 0 4]
           [8 [9 2 10 [13 0 119] 0 3]
              6 [5 [1 0] 0 4]
                [9 2 10 [6 [0 13] 0 5] 0 7]
                0 2]
       0 2]
      6  :: Opcode 3
```

```
[6 [3 0 13]
   [5 [1 3] 0 26] 1 1]
[8 [9 2 10 [13 0 27] 0 1]
 6 [5 [1 0] 0 4]
   [[1 0] 3 0 5]
   0 2]
6  :: Opcode 4
[6 [3 0 13]
   [5 [1 4] 0 26]
   1 1]
[8 [9 2 10 [13 0 27] 0 1]
   6 [5 [1 0] 0 4]
     [6 [6 [3 0 5] [1 1] 1 0]
        [[1 0] 4 0 5]
        1 1.818.845.538 0]
 0 2]
6  :: Opcode 5
[6 [3 0 13]
   [6 [5 [1 5] 0 26] [3 0 27] 1 1] 1 1]
[8 [9 11 10 [29 0 118] 0 1]
   6 [5 [1 0] 0 4]
     [8 [9 2 10 [13 0 119] 0 3]
      6 [5 [1 0] 0 4]
        [[1 0] 5 [0 13] 0 5]
        0 2]
 0 2]
6  :: Opcode 6
[6 [3 0 13]
   [6 [5 [1 6] 0 26]
      [6 [3 0 27] [3 0 55] 1 1] 1 1] 1 1]
[8 [9 11 10 [29 0 118] 0 1]
   6 [5 [1 0] 0 4]
     [6 [5 [1 0] 0 5]
        [9 2 10 [13 0 238] 0 3]
        6 [5 [1 1] 0 5]
          [9 2 10 [13 0 239] 0 3]
          1 1.818.845.538 0]
  0 2]
6  :: Opcode 7
[6 [3 0 13]
   [6 [5 [1 7] 0 26] [3 0 27] 1 1] 1 1]
[8 [9 2 10 [13 0 54] 0 1]
```

```
  6 [5 [1 0] 0 4]
    [9 2 10 [6 [0 5] 0 119] 0 3]
    0 2]
6  :: Opcode 8
[6 [3 0 13]
  [6 [5 [1 8] 0 26] [3 0 27] 1 1] 1 1]
[8 [9 2 10 [13 0 54] 0 1]
  6 [5 [1 0] 0 4]
    [9 2 10 [6 [[0 5] 0 28] 0 119] 0 3]
    0 2]
6  :: Opcode 9
[6 [3 0 13]
  [6 [5 [1 9] 0 26]
    [6 [3 0 27]
      [6 [3 0 54] [1 1] 1 0]
      1 1]
    1 1]
  1 1]
[8 [9 2 10 [13 0 55] 0 1]
  6 [5 [1 0] 0 4]
    [8 [8 [9 22 0 15]
          9 2 10 [6 [0 246] 0 13] 0 2]
    6 [5 [1 0] 0 2]
      [1 1.818.845.538 0]
   9 2 10 [6 [0 13] 0 5]
   0 7]
 0 2]
6  :: Opcode 10
[6 [3 0 13]
  [6 [5 [1 10] 0 26]
    [6 [3 0 27]
      [6 [3 0 54]
        [6 [3 0 108] [1 1] 1 0]
        1 1]
      1 1]
    1 1]
  1 1]
[6 [5 [1 0] 0 108]
  [1 1.818.845.538 0]
  8 [9 2 10 [13 0 55] 0 1]
  6 [5 [1 0] 0 4]
    [8 [9 2 10 [13 0 237] 0 3]
```

```
           6 [5 [1 0] 0 4]
             [8 [8 [9 86 0 31]
                   9 2 10
                   [6 [0 1.004] [0 29] 0 13]
                 0 2]
            6 [5 [1 0] 0 2]
              [1 1.818.845.538 0]
              [1 0]
            0 5]
           0 2]
         0 2]
      6  :: Opcode 11
      [6 [3 0 13]
         [6 [5 [1 11] 0 26]
            [6 [3 0 27]
               [6 [3 0 54]
                  [1 1]
                  1 0]
               1 1]
            1 1]
         1 1]
      [8 [9 2 10 [13 0 55] 0 1]
         6 [5 [1 0] 0 4]
          [[1 0]
            2 [0 28] [1 11] [0 118] [1 1] 0 5]
        0 2]
      1 1.818.845.538 0]
    0 1]
:: +mas
8 [1 0]
  [1 6 [6 [5 [1 3] 0 6] [1 0] 5 [1 2] 0 6]
       [1 1]
       6 [6 [5 [1 1] 0 6] [1 0] 5 [1 0] 0 6]
         [0 0]
         8 [9 20 0 7]
         9 2 10
         [6 [7 [0 3] 7 [8 [9 170 0 7]
                         9 2 10
                         [6 [0 14] 7 [0 3] 1 2]
                         0 2] 0 3]
    7 [0 3] 8 [9 4 0 7]
    9 2 10 [6
```

```
    [7 [0 3]
     9 2 10
     [6 7 [8 [9 170 0 7]
            9 2 10 [6 [0 14] 7 [0 3] 1 2]
            0 2] 0 2]
     0 1]
    7 [0 3] 1 2]
   0 2]
  0 2]
 0 1]
[:: +frag fragmentary subtree of noun
 8 [1 0 0]
  [1 6 [5 [1 0] 0 12]
    [1 0]
    8 [1 6 [5 [1 1] 0 28]
          [[1 0] 0 29]
          6 [6 [3 0 29] [1 1] 1 0]
           [1 0]
           9 2 10
           [14 [8 [9 175 0 15]
                 9 2 10 [6 0 60] 0 2]
            8 [8 [9 342 0 15]
                9 2 10 [6 0 60] 0 2]
            6 [5 [1 2] 0 2]
              [0 122]
              6 [5 [1 3] 0 2]
              [0 123]
              1 1.818.845.538 0]
      0 1]
  9 2 0 1]
 0 1]
[:: +unit, type definition of unit/Maybe
 8
  [8 [1 0] [1 8 [0 6] 8 [5 [0 14] 0 2] 0 6] 0 1]
  [1 8 [1 0]
     [1 8 [6 [3 0 6]
            [[8 [0 30] 9 2 10 [6 0 28] 0 2]
             8 [7 [0 7] 8 [9 46 0 7]
               9 2 10 [6 0 14] 0 2]
             9 2 10 [6 0 29] 0 2]
            6 [5 [1 0] 0 6]
             [1 0]
```

```
                   0 0]
          8 [5 [0 14] 0 2]
          0 6]
      0 1]
    0 1]
  :: +sub subtraction of two atoms
  8 [1 0 0]
    [1 6 [5 [1 0] 0 13]
         [0 12]
         9 2 10
         [6 [8 [9 686 0 7] 9 2 10 [6 0 28] 0 2]
          8 [9 686 0 7] 9 2 10 [6 0 29] 0 2]
    0 1]
  0 1]
0 1]
```

5 Conclusion

Metacircular virtualization is a powerful tool for building interpreters, and Nock is not only no exception, it exemplifies the practice. The design of `++mock` and its underlying `++mink` function provides a practical way to interpret Nock in a way that is both efficient and extensible. One could imagine, for instance, a Nock interpreter cousin to `++mock` that is instrumented for partial evaluation of formulas (as in a debugger or syntax highlighter robust to syntax errors). Nock supports a rich capacity to build metacircular interpreters as a first-class feature, a potential which remains as yet relatively unexplored in the Nock ecosystem. ⌘

References

Amin, Nada and Tiark Rompf (2017). "Collapsing towers of interpreters." In: *Proceedings of the ACM on Programming Languages*. Vol. 2. POPL. New York, NY: Association for Computing Machinery, pp. 1–33. URL: https://doi.org/10.1145/3158140 (visited on ~2025.8.13).

Bawden, Alan (1999). "Quasiquotation in Lisp." In: *Proceedings of the 1999 ACM SIGPLAN workshop on Partial evaluation and semantics-based program manipulation.* New York, NY: Association for Computing Machinery, pp. 4–12. URL: `https://dl.acm.org/doi/10.1145/317636.317640` (visited on ~2025.8.13).

Graham, Paul (2001). "What Made Lisp Different." In: URL: `https://paulgraham.com/diff.html` (visited on ~2025.8.13).

McCarthy, John (1996). *History of Lisp.* URL: `https://www-formal.stanford.edu/jmc/history/lisp/node2.html` (visited on ~2025.8.13).

McCarthy, John and Richard L. Wexelblat (1978). "History of LISP." In: *History of programming languages.* Ed. by Richard L. Wexelblat. New York, NY: Association for Computing Machinery, pp. 173–185. URL: `https://doi.org/10.1145/800025.1198360` (visited on ~2025.8.13).

Sheard, Tim and Simon Peyton Jones (2002). "Template meta-programming for Haskell." In: *Proceedings of the 2002 ACM SIGPLAN workshop on Haskell.* New York, NY: Association for Computing Machinery, pp. 1–16. URL: `https://dl.acm.org/doi/10.1145/581690.581691` (visited on ~2025.8.13).

`~sorreg-namtyv`, Curtis Yarvin (2006) "U, a small model". URL: `http://urbit.sourceforge.net/u.txt` (visited on ~2024.2.20).

— (2010a) "Urbit: functional programming from scratch". URL: `http://moronlab.blogspot.com/2010/01/urbit-functional-programming-from.html` (visited on ~2024.1.25).

— (2010b) "Watt: A Self-Sustaining Functional Language (preprint)". URL: `https://github.com/cgyarvin/urbit/blob/master/Spec/watt/sss10.tex` (visited on ~2025.5.19).

An Implementation of Nock Combinator Logic in Hardware: The NockPU Project

~mopfel-winrux
Native Planet · Southwestern Pool Supply Co.

Abstract

This paper presents the design, implementation, and evaluation of NockPU, a hardware processor that directly executes Nock 4K, a minimalist combinator calculus serving as the foundation for the Urbit computing platform. The research demonstrates the feasibility of implementing all twelve Nock operations in hardware using FPGA-based graph reduction techniques. Key architectural decisions include a cell-based memory representation optimized for 64-bit words, stackless tree traversal using breadcrumb techniques, and integrated Cheney-style copying garbage collection. Performance analysis identifies two primary challenges: excessive memory consumption due to intermediate structure creation during reduction, and computational complexity arising from the graph transformation approach required by combinator reduction. The implemented garbage collector successfully addresses memory consumption issues, preventing system crashes during complex computations. While computational efficiency remains challenging compared to traditional architectures, the NockPU establishes that hardware Nock 4K implementation is viable and provides a foundation for specialized functional computation with advantages in determinism and semantic clarity.

Urbit Systems Technical Journal II:2 (2025): 99–130.
Address author correspondence to ~mopfel-winrux.

Contents

1 Introduction

Combinator calculi represent a fundamental approach to computation based on the application and reduction of combinators – operators that compose and transform data without requiring named variables. Nock is a specific combinator calculus developed as the foundation of Urbit, a clean-slate computing platform. It provides a deterministic, stateless computing environment that trades performance for perfect semantic clarity. While Nock interpreters typically run in software environments (e.g., the C-based Vere interpreter and Rust-based NockVM interpreter for Urbit), little exploration has been done regarding the direct implementation of Nock in hardware.

Implementing Nock in hardware presents unique challenges fundamentally different from traditional assembly languages. While conventional processors operate on byte buffers stored in linear memory arrays, Nock computation operates on *nouns* – recursive tree structures that exist as linked data rather than contiguous memory blocks. This fundamental difference means that traditional hardware architectures, optimized for sequential memory access patterns and fixed-width data types, are poorly suited for the tree traversal and dynamic memory allocation patterns inherent to Nock execution. The challenge lies not merely in implementing the Nock operations themselves, but in developing memory representations and traversal mechanisms that can efficiently handle the recursive, pointer-based data structures that define Nock's computational model.

The motivation behind this research was initially quite straightforward: to address skepticism about whether Nock could be effectively implemented in hardware.

1.1 Related Work and Motivation

Hardware implementation of functional languages has historical precedent, with notable examples including the SKIM (S, K, I reduction machine) developed at Cambridge in the 1970s and more recent work on The Reduceron at the University of York. However, these projects have typically focused on more traditional functional programming languages rather than the minimal, axiomatic approach of Nock. Additionally, most prior research has not sufficiently addressed the challenges of scaling such systems to utilize both on-chip and off-chip memory effectively.

1.2 Project Goals and Approach

This project aimed to answer several key questions:

1. How can Nock's nouns and operations be efficiently represented in hardware memory?
2. What hardware architecture best supports the pattern of execution required by Nock?
3. How can tree traversal be implemented without a stack-based approach?
4. What performance characteristics emerge from a hardware implementation compared to software interpreters?

The primary objective was to build a Verilog-based NockPU that could perform all standard Nock operations, thereby demonstrating the feasibility of hardware-based combinator reduction while identifying optimal design patterns for such an implementation.

2 Background and Related Work

2.1 Nock Specification and Semantics

Nock is a minimalist combinator calculus defined by a small set of axiomatic rules (`~sorreg-namtyv`, 2018). Its specification begins with: "A noun is an atom or a cell. An atom is a natural number. A cell is an ordered pair of nouns." The computational core of Nock is expressed through reduction rules that transform nouns based on operator codes. For example, the reduction rule `*[a 0 b]` performs a slot operation (tree addressing), while `*[a 2 b c]` evaluates `*[*[a b] *[a c]]`, and so forth.

Nock's extreme simplicity makes it an interesting target for hardware implementation. It requires only a handful of operations, has no need for floating-point arithmetic, and functions in a completely deterministic manner (`~sorreg-namtyv` et al.,

2016). Yet, this same simplicity can lead to computational inefficiency when compared to traditional architectures, as Nock requires graph transformations for even basic arithmetic operations.

2.2 Digital Hardware Design Fundamentals

Field-Programmable Gate Arrays (FPGAs) allow for reconfigurable digital hardware design, making them ideal for prototyping novel processor architectures. Unlike traditional software that executes sequentially, hardware designs in languages like Verilog describe circuits where operations occur in parallel, governed by clock cycles.

The design process involves:

1. Creating a high-level design using Hardware Description Language (HDL)
2. Building test benches to verify functionality
3. Synthesis (converting HDL to netlist)
4. Place and Route (mapping netlist to FPGA resources)
5. Timing analysis and program file generation

2.3 Existing Hardware Implementations of Functional Languages

Several significant projects have attempted to implement functional programming languages directly in hardware:

SKIM (S, K, I reduction machine): Developed by Clarke et al. at Cambridge in the 1970s and 1980s (Clarke et al. (1980); Norman, Clarke, and Stoye (1984)), SKIM implemented combinatory logic directly in hardware. It pioneered many of the techniques for graph reduction that influenced later work.

The Reduceron: More recently, work at the University of York by Naylor and Runciman has produced The Reduceron (Naylor and Runciman (2008); Naylor (2009)), an FPGA-based graph reduction machine initially designed for executing Haskell programs using basic combinators (S, K, I, B, C). Later versions moved to more complex supercombinator implementations.

While these implementations provide valuable precedent, they differ from the NockPU in several important ways:

1. They primarily target conventional functional languages rather than a minimal combinator calculus like Nock
2. They typically employ stack-based reduction strategies
3. They have focused less on scalability across on-chip and off-chip memory boundaries

2.4 Stack-based vs. Stackless Architectures

Traditional approaches to traversing tree structures in hardware often rely on stack-based mechanisms, wherein a stack stores return addresses or intermediate state during traversal. While intuitive, this approach can introduce complexity in hardware implementation and potentially limit parallelism.

The stackless approach, in contrast, embeds navigational information directly within the tree structure itself, allowing for traversal without external stack state. This technique requires careful consideration of how to mark nodes during traversal and how to restore the tree to its original form afterward, but can offer advantages in certain hardware contexts.

2.5 Memory Representation Challenges in Functional Computing

Representing functional data structures efficiently in memory presents several challenges. Traditional memory is organized as a linear array of words, while functional data often takes the form of trees or graphs. Additionally, functional programs frequently create and discard temporary structures during evaluation, necessitating effective memory management strategies.

In hardware implementations, memory access patterns significantly impact performance. On-chip memory offers fast access but limited capacity, while off-chip memory provides greater capacity at the cost of higher latency. Effective design must carefully balance these tradeoffs.

3 NockPU Architecture

3.1 System Overview and Design Philosophy

The NockPU is designed as a specialized processor that directly executes Nock operations in hardware. Its architecture emphasizes several key principles:

1. **Memory-centric design**: Since combinator reduction is fundamentally about memory manipulation, the architecture prioritizes efficient memory operations.
2. **Deterministic execution**: The system maintains Nock's deterministic nature, ensuring consistent results for identical inputs.
3. **Stackless traversal**: Rather than relying on a traditional stack for tree traversal, the NockPU embeds traversal state within the memory structure itself.
4. **Scalability across memory boundaries**: The design accommodates both on-chip and off-chip memory, allowing for larger computations than could fit in on-chip memory alone.

Figure 1 illustrates the overall system architecture of the NockPU, showing the interconnections between its major components. The Memory Traversal Unit serves as the central coordinator, managing communication between the execution subsystems and memory hierarchy. The architecture demonstrates a clear separation between control logic, execution units, and memory management, enabling modular design and efficient resource utilization.

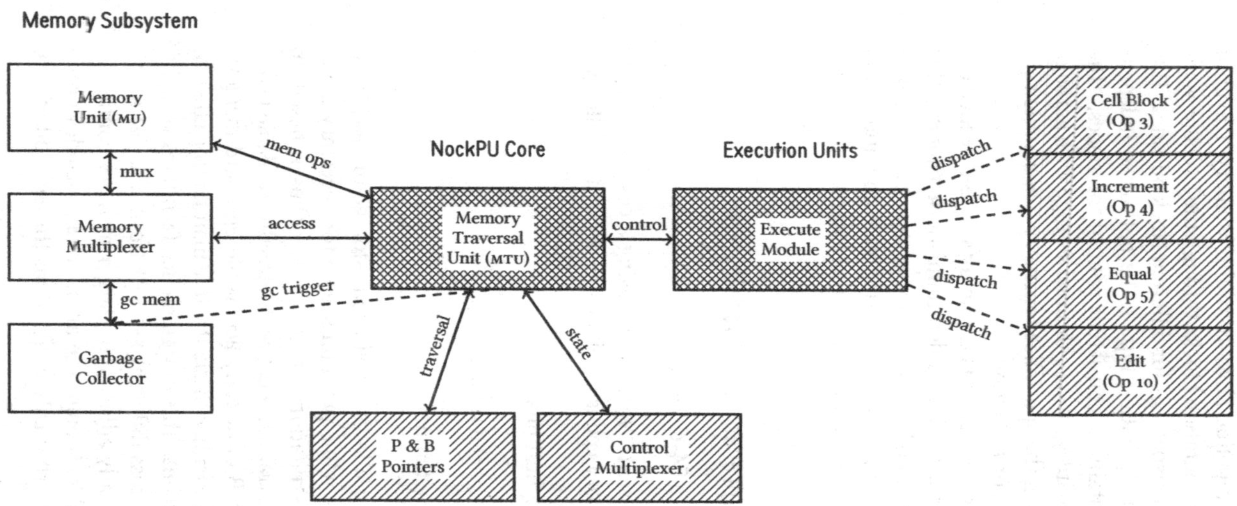

Figure 1: NockPU System Architecture Overview. The Memory Traversal Unit serves as the central controller, coordinating between execution modules and memory management components. Specialized operation blocks handle specific Nock opcodes, while the memory subsystem provides cell-based storage with integrated garbage collection. Bidirectional arrows (solid) indicate control and data flow, while one-way arrows (dashed) show dispatch operations.

The execution pipeline flows from the Memory Traversal Unit to specialized operation blocks through the Execute Module, which acts as a dispatcher for different Nock opcodes. This design allows each operation type to be optimized independently while maintaining consistent control interfaces. The memory subsystem integrates traditional storage with garbage collection, providing the specialized memory management required for combinator reduction.

The architecture implements explicitly single-threaded execution, consistent with Nock's deterministic semantics. This design choice ensures that all computations proceed in a predictable, sequential manner, eliminating race conditions and maintaining the mathematical purity that characterizes Nock evaluation.

3.2 Memory Representation Model

3.2.1 28-bit Nouns in 64-bit Words

The NockPU represents Nock nouns using a custom memory format. Each memory cell is 64 bits wide, divided as follows:

- 8 tag bits (highest bits)
- 28 bits for the head noun
- 28 bits for the tail noun

This representation allows for efficient storage of Nock's binary tree structure while providing room for necessary metadata. The 28-bit limitation for nouns was chosen based on practical FPGA constraints: most commercially available FPGAS have at most 256MB of directly accessible on-board memory, making 28-bit addressing sufficient while maintaining efficient 64-bit word alignment. This design choice facilitates straightforward scaling across different FPGA platforms, as the architecture can be trivially adjusted for larger memory configurations when available, though the architecture includes provisions for handling arbitrarily large atoms through linked representations.

3.2.2 Tag Bit Utilization

Tag bits represent auxiliary metadata embedded within memory words to support architectural features beyond basic data storage. In traditional von Neumann architectures, such metadata is typically maintained in separate control structures or registers. However, the NockPU's specialized design for combinator reduction necessitates embedding control information directly within the memory representation to enable efficient stackless traversal and cell-based addressing.

The NockPU's tag bit architecture serves several critical functions essential for hardware-based functional computation. The stackless tree traversal mechanism requires embedding traversal state within memory cells themselves, using dedicated bits to track which branches have been visited during tree navigation. The cell-addressed memory model demands type information to distinguish between atoms and cells at the hardware level. Additionally, execution control bits mark cells requiring evaluation, while reserved bits provide extensibility for future architectural enhancements.

Table 1 provides a complete specification of the 8-bit tag field structure used in the NockPU's 64-bit memory words. Each tag bit serves a specific architectural purpose, from execution control to traversal state management, enabling the processor to maintain the semantic clarity of Nock computation while achieving practical hardware implementation.

Table 1: NockPU Tag Bits Layout (Bits 63–56)

Bit	Name	Explanation
63	Execute	Marks cell as requiring execution
62	Stack	Contains operation code and operand
61	Reserved	Reserved for future extensions
60	Large Atom	Atom larger than 28 bits
59	Head Traversal	Tracks head traversal state
58	Tail Traversal	Tracks tail traversal state
57	Head Tag	Head is atom (0) or cell (1)
56	Tail Tag	Tail is atom (0) or cell (1)

Example: The Nock cell `[42 43]` is represented as a 64-bit word with the following bits:

Tag bits (63–56):	00000011_2 (both head and tail are atoms)
Head (55–28):	$0x000002A_2$ (28-bit representation of 42)
Tail (27–0):	$0x000002B_2$ (28-bit representation of 43)
Complete word:	$0x03000002A000002B_2$

3.2.3 Atom and Cell Representation

In the NockPU memory model, atoms (natural numbers) are represented directly within the 28-bit fields when possible. For atoms that exceed this limit, the system can use multiple memory cells linked together.

Cells are represented as pointers to other memory locations. When both the head and tail of a cell are direct atoms, they can be stored directly within a single memory word. When either is a cell, the corresponding field contains a pointer to another memory location.

3.3 Stackless Tree Traversal Mechanism

3.3.1 Program Pointer and Back Pointer Methodology

The NockPU implements a stackless approach to tree traversal (Burrows, 2009) using two primary pointers:

1. **Program Pointer (P)**: Points to the current node being processed
2. **Back Pointer (B)**: Points to the previous node in the traversal

Together, these pointers allow the system to navigate the tree structure without requiring a separate stack. The approach fundamentally works by leaving "breadcrumbs" in the form of modified pointers that enable retracing steps back up the tree after descending.

3.3.2 Breadcrumb Trail Implementation

The stackless traversal mechanism operates by temporarily modifying tree pointers to create navigational breadcrumbs, as demonstrated in Figure 2. This approach eliminates the need for external stack memory while maintaining the ability to navigate complex tree structures during Nock evaluation.

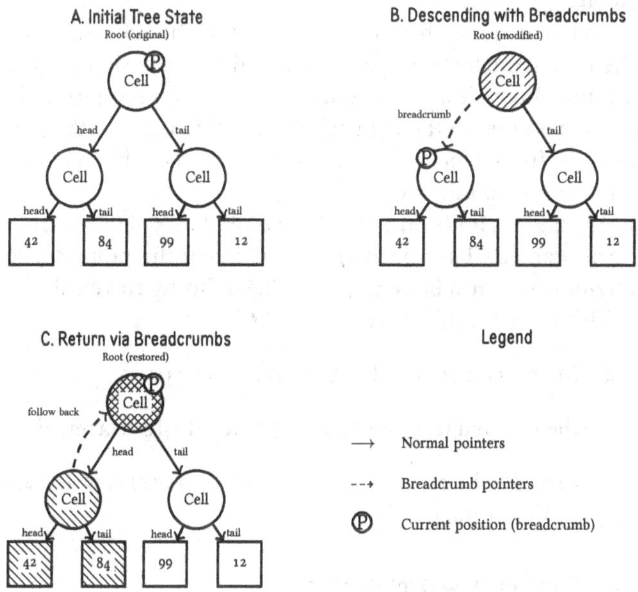

Figure 2: Stackless Tree Traversal Sequence demonstrating breadcrumb-based navigation without a traditional call stack. The NockPU implements tree traversal without a stack by modifying pointers to create breadcrumb trails. Sequence:

A. Initial tree state with root and subtrees.
B. Descend into the left subtree leaving breadcrumb.
C. Follow breadcrumb back to root to continue with right.

The traversal sequence shown in the figure illustrates the three-phase operation: initialization, descent with breadcrumb creation, and return via breadcrumb following. In subfigure

A, the tree exists in its canonical form with normal pointer relationships. Subfigure B shows the critical breadcrumb creation phase, where the processor modifies the root cell's head pointer to store a return path before descending into the left subtree. Subfigure C demonstrates the return mechanism, in which the breadcrumb is followed back to the root, restoring the original pointer structure while marking the left subtree as visited.

As the processor traverses the tree, it modifies the memory cells it visits, effectively leaving a trail that can be followed back up. When descending into a subtree, the processor redirects the pointer in the left part of the cell to point to the parent node, from which execution flow just came. This creates a pathway back up the tree.

The tag bits for head and tail traversal (bits 59 and 58) track which branches have been visited, allowing the processor to determine which subtree to explore next during traversal.

This mechanism ensures that:

1. The processor can always retrace its steps
2. The original tree can be reconstructed after traversal
3. Shared subtrees remain unmodified, preserving the integrity of the graph

3.4 Control Flow Architecture

3.4.1 Memory Traversal Control

The Memory Traversal Unit (MTU) serves as the master controller for the NockPU, orchestrating the overall execution flow. It performs several key functions:

1. Initiates tree traversal to find nodes marked for execution
2. Maintains the program and back pointers
3. Passes control to specialized execution modules when appropriate

4. Coordinates memory access through the memory multiplexer

The MTU operates according to a finite state machine that manages the complex coordination between memory operations, tree traversal, and execution control. The state machine includes states for memory access initiation, traversal coordination, execution delegation, and result handling. State transitions are triggered by completion signals from subordinate modules, memory operation acknowledgments, and the detection of execution markers within the traversed tree structure. This state-driven approach ensures that all memory operations complete properly before proceeding and that control flow remains deterministic throughout the computation process.

3.4.2 Execute Module

The Execute module handles the reduction of Nock operations when triggered by the MTU. It receives the address and data for a cell marked for execution, performs the appropriate transformation according to the Nock operation code, and returns control to the MTU when complete.

This module contains specialized logic for each Nock operator (0 through 11), implementing their specific reduction rules. For operators that generate nested executions, the Execute module restructures the memory to reflect the transformed computation and marks the relevant cells for future execution.

3.4.3 Operational Modules

In addition to the core Execute module, the NockPU includes several specialized modules for specific operations:

- **Cell Block**: Handle type checking for the cell operator (opcode 3)
- **Increment Block**: Implement increment operations (opcode 4)
- **Equal Block**: Perform equality comparisons (opcode 5)

- **Edit Block**: Handle tree modification for the replace operator (opcode 10)

These specialized modules allow for more efficient implementation of specific operations and better utilization of hardware parallelism.

3.4.4 Error Handling and System Integrity

The NockPU includes a comprehensive error detection and reporting system to maintain system integrity during execution. When an error condition is encountered—such as malformed nouns, invalid operation codes, or memory access violations—the system raises an error signal and provides diagnostic information through an error code bus. This approach allows for graceful error handling while maintaining the deterministic nature of Nock execution, ensuring that invalid computations are detected rather than producing undefined results.

3.4.5 Garbage Collection Implementation

The NockPU implements a Cheney-style copying garbage collector based on the algorithm described by Clark (1976). This implementation addresses the significant memory consumption challenges inherent in combinator reduction by reclaiming memory occupied by intermediate structures that are no longer reachable.

The garbage collection process operates as follows:

1. **Traversal Reset**: Before initiating garbage collection, the system resets any active tree traversal state, ensuring that breadcrumb modifications are properly unwound and the memory representation returns to its canonical form.

2. **Copying Phase**: Using Cheney's two-space copying algorithm, reachable nouns are copied from the current memory space to a clean memory partition, with pointer updates maintaining referential integrity.

3. **Space Flip**: Once copying is complete, the roles of the two memory spaces are exchanged, making the compacted space the active working memory.

A key advantage of this design is that computation state does not need to be recreated after garbage collection. Since the NockPU's execution model is based on marking cells for execution rather than maintaining complex execution stacks, the collector can preserve all necessary computational context during the copying process. This allows garbage collection to occur transparently without requiring expensive state reconstruction. The tradeoff is that the traversal reset process takes some clock cycles, but this approach eliminates the need to maintain extra state during garbage collection.

The copying collector approach is particularly well-suited to the NockPU's stackless architecture, as it eliminates the need to traverse and update complex stack structures during collection. The collector operates entirely through memory scanning and pointer updating, maintaining compatibility with the breadcrumb-based traversal mechanism used throughout the system.

4 Implementation Details

4.1 Hardware Design Process and Tools

4.1.1 Verilog Implementation

The NockPU was implemented in Verilog, a hardware description language that allows for precise control over the digital circuit design. The implementation follows a modular approach, with separate components for different functional aspects of the processor.

Key Verilog modules include:

- Memory Unit (`memory_unit.v`)
- Memory Traversal Unit (`mem_traversal.v`)
- Execute Module (`execute.v`)

- Specialized Operation Blocks
- Memory Multiplexer (`memory_mux.v`)
- Control Multiplexer (`control_mux.v`)

Each module was designed with clear interfaces and tested independently before integration.

4.1.2 Testing and Verification Methodology

A comprehensive testing framework was developed to verify the correctness of the NockPU implementation across multiple levels of abstraction:

End-to-End Testing: The primary verification approach uses an end-to-end test bench (`execute_tb`) that inputs known Nock formulas and compares the resulting output with a reference Nock interpreter. This approach ensures semantic equivalence between the hardware implementation and established software interpreters, validating that the NockPU produces correct results for complete Nock programs.

Component-Level Testing: Individual subsystems are verified through dedicated test benches:

- Memory traversal test bench: Verifies the correctness of the stackless tree traversal mechanism, ensuring proper navigation and breadcrumb management
- Memory operations test bench: Validates basic memory read, write, and allocation operations across the bisected memory architecture

This modular testing approach allows for isolation of functionality and systematic debugging, enabling verification of both individual components and their integration. The test benches provide comprehensive coverage of the processor's operational modes and edge cases, ensuring robust implementation of the Nock specification.

4.2 Nock Operation Implementation

4.2.1 Basic Operations (Slot, Constant)

The simplest Nock operations are implemented directly within the memory traversal and execution modules:

Slot Operation (`*[a 0 b]`) Implemented by traversing the subject tree according to the address pattern specified by `b`. The implementation uses a bit-wise approach where each bit in the address determines whether to follow the head or tail pointer.

Constant Operation (`*[a 1 b]`) Simply returns the constant `b` regardless of the subject. This is implemented by writing the value of `b` directly to the result cell.

4.2.2 Tree Manipulation Operations

Operations that transform the tree structure are implemented through carefully orchestrated memory manipulations:

Evaluation (`*[a 2 b c]`) Constructs a new tree representing `*[*[a b] *[a c]]`, marking the appropriate cells for execution. This operation demonstrates the NockPU's approach to graph transformation, where complex Nock operations are implemented by restructuring memory to reflect the semantically equivalent expanded form.

Figure 3 illustrates the memory transformation process for Nock opcode 2, showing how the original nested structure is converted into separate evaluation branches. The transformation allocates new memory cells (addresses `0x09` and `0x0A`) to represent the two evaluation paths `*[a b]` and `*[a c]`, while preserving the original subject data at address `0x02`. The execute bits (`0x80` in the tag field) mark the newly created cells for evaluation, allowing the processor to continue the reduction process on the transformed structure.

This approach exemplifies the NockPU's philosophy of implementing complex operations through memory restructuring rather than traditional control flow. The deterministic na-

Before: Memory State for
`*[[50 51] [2 [0 3] [1 [4 0 1]]]]`

Address	Tag Bits	Head	Tail
0x00	0x00	0x0000000	0x0000009
0x01	0x80	0x0000002	0x0000003
0x02	0x03	**0x0000032**	**0x0000033**
0x03	0x02	<u>0x0000002</u>	0x0000004
0x04	0x00	0x0000005	0x0000006
0x05	0x03	<u>0x0000000</u>	**0x0000003**
0x06	0x02	<u>0x0000001</u>	0x0000007
0x07	0x02	<u>0x0000004</u>	0x0000008
0x08	0x02	<u>0x0000000</u>	**0x0000001**

After: Memory State for
`*[*[[50 51] [0 3]] *[[50 51] [1 [4 0 1]]]]`

Address	Tag Bits	Head	Tail
0x00	0x00	0x0000000	0x0000009
0x01	0x80	0x0000009	0x000000A
0x02	0x03	**0x0000032**	**0x0000033**
0x03	0x02	<u>0x0000002</u>	0x0000004
0x04	0x00	0x0000005	0x0000006
0x05	0x03	<u>0x0000000</u>	**0x0000003**
0x06	0x02	<u>0x0000001</u>	0x0000007
0x07	0x02	<u>0x0000004</u>	0x0000008
0x08	0x02	<u>0x0000000</u>	**0x0000001**
0x09	0x80	0x0000002	0x0000005
0x0A	0x80	0x0000002	0x0000006

Key:

- **`Bold value`**: Data atom (direct value like 50, 51, 3, 1)
- <u>`Underlined value`</u>: Opcode (like Nock 2, 0, 4)
- `Normal value`: Pointer to memory location
- `Grayed cell` : Memory address that has been modified

Figure 3: Memory transformation for Nock opcode 2 (Evaluation) demonstrating the conversion from opcode structure to evaluation branches, showing how `*[a 2 b c]` becomes `*[*[a b] *[a c]]` through memory graph restructuring.

ture of memory allocation ensures consistent behavior, while the tagging system provides the execution control necessary for proper evaluation sequencing.

Cell Testing (`*[a 3 b]`) Examines whether the result of `*[a b]` is a cell, returning the appropriate truth value.

Increment (`*[a 4 b]`) Increments the result of `*[a b]` by one, using specialized logic.

Equality (`*[a 5 b c]`) Compares the results of `*[a b]` and `*[a c]` for equality.

4.2.3 Conditional Operation Implementation

The conditional operation (`*[a 6 b c d]`) is particularly challenging due to its branching nature. In the NockPU, it is implemented by constructing the equivalent expression

```
*[a *[[c d] 0 *[[2 3] 0 *[a 4 4 b]]]]
```

directly in memory.

This approach, while computationally expensive, maintains semantic equivalence with the Nock specification and demonstrates how even complex operations can be expressed through graph transformation rather than traditional control flow.

4.2.4 Composition, Push, and Call Operations

Operations 7, 8, and 9 share a common implementation pattern in the NockPU: they perform graph reduction by writing the equivalent expanded expression directly into memory, then rely on the normal execution order to evaluate the result correctly.

Composition (`*[a 7 b c]`) The NockPU writes the graph reduction `*[*[a b] c]` directly into memory. The normal execution order ensures that `*[a b]` is evaluated first, with its result becoming the subject for the subsequent evaluation of `c`.

Push (`*[a 8 b c]`) Implemented by writing the expansion `*[[*[a b] a] c]` into memory. The execution system constructs a cell containing both the result of `*[a b]` and the original subject `a`, creating the augmented context needed for evaluating `c`.

Call (`*[a 9 b c]`) Constructs the graph reduction `*[*[a c] 2 [0 1] 0 b]` in memory. This creates the function call frame structure, with normal execution order ensuring proper evaluation sequence: first `*[a c]` to obtain the function, then the constructed evaluation context.

This unified approach eliminates the need for specialized control flow logic in hardware. Instead, the NockPU leverages its graph reduction capabilities and the inherent ordering properties of the traversal mechanism to achieve correct execution semantics for all three operations.

4.2.5 Edit Operation Implementation

The edit operation (`*[a 10 [b c] d]`) performs tree modification through the specialized Edit Block module. This operation implements the tree editing function `#[b *[a c] *[a d]]`, which modifies the tree structure at address `b` by replacing the value with the result of `*[a c]` and continuing evaluation with `*[a d]`.

The Edit Block uses careful pointer manipulation to modify tree structures while preserving shared subtrees and maintaining memory consistency. This operation requires sophisticated address calculation and memory management to ensure that tree modifications do not corrupt other parts of the computation.

4.2.6 Hint Operation Implementation

The hint operation (`*[a 11 [b c] d]`) provides optimization opportunities by transforming to `*[[*[a c] *[a d]] 0 3]`. While semantically equivalent to its expansion, hints in the NockPU architecture are designed to enable hardware-specific optimizations or jetting.

The current implementation constructs the hint structure in memory and proceeds with standard evaluation. However, the architecture includes provisions for recognizing specific hint patterns that could be accelerated through specialized hardware modules or optimized execution paths, representing a key area for future performance improvements.

4.3 Memory Management

4.3.1 Heap Allocation Strategy

The NockPU employs a heap-based memory allocation strategy. A free memory chain links together all available memory cells, and operations claim cells from this chain as needed. The free memory pointer (`F`) tracks the next available cell.

This approach allows for dynamic allocation without requiring complex memory management hardware, albeit at the cost of potential fragmentation over time.

4.3.2 Memory Access Patterns

The memory architecture is designed to optimize the prevalent access patterns in Nock execution:

1. **Cell-Based Memory Model**: Each memory word represents a complete cell containing both head and tail components within the 64-bit word structure. Single atoms are represented as cells `[a NIL]`, where `NIL` is the maximum direct atom value (28-bits).

2. **Parallel Memory Operations**: The design allows up to three memory operations per processor cycle: two reads and one write, enabling efficient traversal and manipulation of tree structures.

3. **Memory Management Unit (MMU)**: The NockPU is shielded from off-chip memory complexity through an MMU that handles the translation between the processor's cell-based addressing and the underlying memory hierarchy.

5 Evaluation and Analysis

The NockPU evaluation encompasses both functional verification and performance analysis to assess the viability of hardware-based Nock execution. Testing methodology focuses on semantic equivalence validation through comparison with reference implementations, while performance analysis examines execution characteristics, memory usage patterns, and computational complexity across representative benchmark programs. The evaluation identifies both the capabilities and limitations of the current implementation, providing a foundation for understanding the tradeoffs inherent in hardware combinator reduction.

5.1 Test Methodology

5.1.1 Test Bench Design

A comprehensive test bench was developed to evaluate the NockPU's functionality and performance. The test bench allows for loading different Nock programs into memory, executing them, and analyzing the results.

The testing framework includes:

- Memory initialization from hex files
- Execution control and timing
- Result validation
- Performance measurement through cycle counting

5.1.2 Operation Verification

Each Nock operation was verified through specific test cases designed to exercise different aspects of its functionality. Waveform analysis allowed for detailed examination of the processor's behavior during execution, ensuring correctness and identifying potential optimization opportunities.

5.2 Performance Metrics

Performance benchmarking of the NockPU was conducted using representative Nock operations that exercise different aspects of the hardware architecture. The test configuration utilized a total memory allocation of 2048 words, split equally between active and garbage collection spaces (1024 words each), running at a 50MHz clock frequency. This memory constraint significantly impacts performance characteristics due to the frequency of garbage collection cycles required during computation.

The benchmark suite encompasses operations ranging from simple arithmetic to complex recursive functions, providing insight into the computational complexity of hardware-based combinator reduction. Table 2 presents comprehensive performance data for these representative operations, demonstrating the relationship between computational complexity and execution time in the NockPU architecture.

Table 2: NockPU performance metrics for 50MHz clock and 16KB memory

Operation	Input	Cycles	Time
Decrement	n=3	32,640	652.8 μs
Decrement	n=10	110,137	2.20 ms
Ackermann	A(1,2)	1,214,348	24.29 ms
Ackermann	A(1,3)	1,782,038	35.64 ms
Ackermann	A(2,1)	3,266,189	65.32 ms
Ackermann	A(2,2)	6,533,725	130.67 ms
Equality	`*[50 5 [0 1] 0 1]`	406	8.12 μs
Equality	`*[[99 99] 5 [0 1] 0 1]`	479	9.58 μs
Addition	`(add 2 2)`	116,310	2.33 ms
Addition	`(add 4 4)`	253,917	5.08 ms
Slot	Depth 3	164	3.27 μs
Slot	Depth 7	156	3.12 μs

The benchmark results reveal several key performance characteristics of the NockPU architecture. Simple operations such as equality testing complete in hundreds of cycles, while complex recursive operations like the Ackermann function require millions of cycles due to extensive intermediate structure creation. The 1024-word memory constraint creates a distinctive "step function" behavior in the computational complexity analysis: when operations exceed available memory, garbage collection cycles introduce significant overhead, causing performance to degrade in discrete steps rather than smooth progression.

This memory-bounded performance profile is particularly evident in recursive operations, where the combination of exponential intermediate structure growth and periodic garbage collection creates compound performance effects. The deterministic nature of the architecture ensures consistent timing for identical operations, but the interplay between memory consumption and collection cycles makes performance prediction dependent on both algorithmic complexity and memory utilization patterns. These characteristics distinguish the NockPU's performance profile from traditional architectures, where performance typically scales more predictably with computational complexity.

5.3 Limitations and Challenges

5.3.1 Memory Consumption Issues

The most significant limitation initially encountered was excessive memory consumption due to the creation of intermediate structures during reduction. Early testing revealed that even moderately complex programs would quickly exhaust available memory without proper memory management.

For instance, a decrement operation on the number 10 would crash the system due to memory exhaustion. This limitation led to the implementation of the Cheney-style copying garbage collector described in Section 3.4.5, which successfully addresses these memory management challenges by reclaiming unreachable intermediate structures and maintaining system stability during complex computations.

5.3.2 Performance Bottlenecks

Several performance bottlenecks were identified:

1. **Memory Access Latency**: Particularly when using off-chip memory, which is significantly slower than on-chip memory.
2. **Sequential Reduction**: The inherently sequential nature of certain reduction patterns limits parallelism.
3. **Tree Traversal Overhead**: The need to navigate complex tree structures introduces overhead compared to direct operations.

5.3.3 Conditional Operation Overhead

The implementation of the conditional operation `*[a 6 b c d]` proved particularly inefficient due to its expression as a complex tree transformation rather than a simple branch. This approach, while semantically pure, introduces significant overhead compared to traditional conditional execution.

6 Future Work

6.1 Arbitrary-size Atom Support

While the current implementation supports 28-bit atoms, supporting arbitrarily large atoms is necessary for full Nock compatibility. The proposed implementation uses a structured approach where large atoms are represented as follows:

- **Header Cell**: The head contains the length of the large atom, while the tail serves as workspace for the interpreter.
- **Data Storage**: The address immediately following the header contains the first 64 bits of the large atom in little-endian format, with subsequent addresses containing additional 64-bit segments as needed.

This design requires specific modifications to atom-manipulating operations:

1. **Increment Operation**: Must reallocate the entire large atom and perform increment with carry propagation across all 64-bit segments, ensuring proper handling of size changes when carries extend the atom length.
2. **Comparison Operations**: Equality testing must traverse the complete atom representation, comparing both length and all data segments to ensure accurate results.
3. **Garbage Collection**: The existing Cheney-style collector can handle large atoms naturally by copying the header and all associated data segments during the copying phase, with no fundamental changes to the collection algorithm.

The memory allocation system remains unchanged, as large atoms are allocated as contiguous blocks following the header cell.

6.2 Hardware Jetting Strategy

"Jetting" refers to the replacement of inefficient Nock code patterns with optimized implementations. A promising approach for hardware jetting involves using a secondary processor that:

1. Detects specific patterns in the Nock code
2. Executes optimized hardware implementations
3. Returns results to the main NockPU

This hybrid approach could dramatically improve performance for common operations while maintaining semantic equivalence with pure Nock.

7 Discussion and Implications

7.1 Theoretical Implications for Computer Architecture

The NockPU project provides insights into the relationship between computation models and hardware architecture. Traditional von Neumann architectures are optimized for imperative, state-based computation, while the NockPU represents an approach tailored for functional, stateless computation.

This work suggests that specialized architectures for specific computational paradigms may offer advantages over general-purpose solutions in certain contexts. The NockPU's design choices, such as the stackless traversal mechanism and integrated garbage collection, illustrate how hardware can be adapted to better support the patterns inherent in combinator reduction.

7.2 Practical Applications

7.2.1 Low-power Computing

The deterministic nature of Nock, combined with the potential power efficiency of specialized hardware, suggests applications in low-power computing environments where predictability is valued over raw performance.

Preliminary analysis suggests that a dedicated NockPU could offer significant power efficiency advantages over general-purpose CPUs running Nock interpreters. The specialized nature of the architecture eliminates much of the overhead associated with general-purpose instruction decoding, branch prediction, and speculative execution. Additionally, the deterministic execution model prevents the power consumption variability that characterizes modern CPUs with dynamic frequency scaling and complex power management.

Future work should include comprehensive power analysis and optimization of the architecture for low-power operation, particularly focusing on minimizing memory access energy and optimizing the garbage collection process for power efficiency.

7.2.2 Verifiable Computing

The simplicity and determinism of the NockPU architecture could make it easier to formally verify than complex general-purpose CPUs, opening possibilities for applications requiring high assurance of correctness.

The limited instruction set, deterministic execution model, and absence of speculative execution or complex branch prediction reduce the verification burden compared to modern processors. Applications in safety-critical systems, cryptographic processing, or environments requiring audit trails could benefit from this simplified verification process. However, the practical deployment of such systems would need to balance the verification advantages against the performance limitations inherent in the current implementation.

7.3 Comparison with Traditional Architectures

When compared to traditional CPU architectures, the NockPU reveals fundamental tradeoffs:

1. **Performance vs. Simplicity**: The NockPU sacrifices raw performance for semantic clarity and simplicity.
2. **Flexibility vs. Specialization**: General-purpose CPUs offer flexibility across computing paradigms, while the NockPU is specialized for combinator reduction.
3. **Memory Efficiency vs. Semantic Purity**: The NockPU's approach to computation requires more memory operations than optimized imperative code.

These tradeoffs suggest that the NockPU and similar architectures may find their niche in specialized applications rather than general-purpose computing.

8 Conclusion

The NockPU project has successfully demonstrated the feasibility of implementing the Nock combinator calculus directly in hardware, providing concrete architectural solutions for functional computation while identifying the fundamental challenges inherent to combinator reduction.

This work presents a complete hardware implementation of Nock using established techniques adapted for combinator reduction. The stackless tree traversal mechanism enables efficient navigation of Nock's recursive tree structures without external stack management. The cell-based memory representation optimizes 64-bit words for Nock's binary tree structures, with 28-bit nouns and 8 tag bits providing efficient metadata management. The integration of Cheney-style copying garbage collection directly into the processor architecture demonstrates that memory management can be successfully embedded as a hardware feature rather than remaining a software concern.

The research identifies two primary challenges to efficient hardware Nock execution: excessive memory consumption due to intermediate structure creation during combinator reduction, and computational complexity arising from the graph transformation approach required by Nock's semantic model. The first challenge is successfully addressed through the implemented garbage collector, which prevents system crashes and maintains stability during complex computations. The second remains an area for future optimization.

The implementation demonstrates that all twelve Nock operations can be realized in hardware through graph reduction techniques, establishing a complete foundation for Nock computation. While computational efficiency remains challenging, the core architectural approach—particularly the integration of garbage collection and cell-based memory management—provides a viable foundation for specialized functional computation that offers advantages in determinism and semantic clarity over general-purpose architectures.

Acknowledgments

The author would like to thank `~master-morzod` and `~fodwyt-ragful` for helping with many technical questions and `~mister-todteg` for funding this development.

References

Burrows, E. (2009). "A Combinator Processor." In: *Part II Computer Science Tripos.*

Clark, Douglas W. (1976). "An Efficient List-Moving Algorithm Using Constant Workspace." In: *Communications of the ACM* 19.6, pp. 352–354. DOI: 10.1145/360238.360249.

Clarke, T. J. W. et al. (1980). "SKIM—The S, K, I Reduction Machine." In: *Proceedings of the 1980 ACM Conference on LISP and Functional Programming.* New York City, NY: ACM, pp. 128–135. DOI: 10.1145/800087.802799.

Naylor, Matthew (2009). "Hardware-Assisted and Target-Directed Evaluation of Functional Programs." PhD thesis. York, United Kingdom: University of York.

Naylor, Matthew and Colin Runciman (2008). "The Reduceron: Widening the von Neumann Bottleneck for Graph Reduction Using an FPGA." In: *Implementation and Application of Functional Languages.* Vol. 5083. Lecture Notes in Computer Science. Springer, pp. 129–146.

Norman, A. C., T. J. W. Clarke, and W. R. Stoye (1984). "Some Practical Methods for Rapid Combinator Reduction." In: *Proceedings of the 1984 ACM Symposium on LISP and Functional Programming.* New York City, NY: ACM, pp. 159–166. DOI: 10.1145/800055.802036.

~sorreg-namtyv, Curtis Yarvin (2018) "Nock 4K". URL: https://docs.urbit.org/language/nock/reference/definition (visited on ~2024.2.20).

~sorreg-namtyv, Curtis Yarvin et al. (2016). *Urbit: A Solid-State Interpreter.* Whitepaper. Tlon Corporation. URL: https://media.urbit.org/whitepaper.pdf (visited on ~2024.1.25).

Notes on Vases

N. E. Davis `~lagrev-nocfep`
Zorp Corp

Abstract

This paper explores the concept of "vases" in the Hoon programming language, an approach to managing type dynamically in a static environment. Vases find applications throughout Nock solid-state systems, including compilation, metaprogramming, and dynamic code evaluation. We will explore how vases are constructed, manipulated, and utilized in the context of Nock and Hoon, providing a foundation for understanding their role in Urbit's programming ecosystem.

Contents

Urbit Systems Technical Journal II:2 (2025): 131–153.
Address author correspondence to ~lagrev-nocfep.

1 Introduction

Nock is homoiconic and only recognizes natural numbers or "atoms" (nonnegative integers, $\mathbb{Z}^*$) and pairs or "cells", as values. Although Nock is untyped, it is desirable to build typed languages targeting this instruction set architecture.

The Hoon programming language solves this by using a pair of a type description and a noun, or raw Nock value. In some ways like a macro over Nock, Hoon introduces static typing (thus extending from Nock's exclusive use of natural numbers) and other design patterns convenient to programmers.[1] Most of the time, developers work in "static Hoon", which maintains guard rails and is easier to reason about. However, a more flexible and powerful modality is available. The type description, or type of the subject, contains information like variable names, variable types, aliases, and the overall structure of the execution environment. Essentially, it acts as a strictly defined metadata reference set for the associated Nock value and its execution environment. We call such a pair of type and

[1] The Jock language does not directly expose vases for utilization, but does utilize them inside the compiler, written in Hoon.

value a "vase".[2] Most commonly used in building code and in manipulating vanes, vases permit the developer to edit the type and the value directly. Essentially, a value can be lifted from a static Hoon context into a dynamic vase context, then reduced back to static Hoon or untyped Nock.

Vase mode, then, describes a design pattern for lifting statically-typed values from their normal compile-time world into a dynamically-typed operating environment, which is then used to produced valid and validated Nock ISA code while enforcing the Hoon language type constraints. Vase mode is used in building compilers, interpreters, and code imports. Since code is transmitted as a noun value to be built and executed on the receiver's side, this also affects hotloading code and system upgrades. A vase algebra describes how to combine the type subject information and the associated value information, as in an import or a REPL. This lets Hoon have human-legible affordances in type and validation, while retaining a simple target ISA for execution, code proving, and optimized execution.[3]

2 Hoon Compilation in a Nutshell

Before we can really grasp the utility of vase mode, we require a brief diversion into how Hoon code is actually compiled and built into Nock. That is, given a Hoon expression, how do we get it into a form that can be executed by the Nock virtual machine? A number of convenience functions wrap various parts of the Hoon compiler, which primarily consists of `+vast` and `+ut`.

Text→Nock . To evaluate a string containing Hoon directly, one merely needs to `+make` the `cord` (text atom).[4]

---

[2]Different interpreters and compilers call this pair different things. For instance, CPython calls this a "boxed value" and keeps the value as a pair of datum and type tag.

[3]A vase visualization tool has been produced by `~migrev-dolseg`, available at `https://hawk.computer`.

[4]Note that Nock instructions are marked as constants with `%` for legibility, but the value is simply the associated integer.

```
> (make '~[1 2 3]')
[%1 p=[1 2 3 0]]

> (make '=+(a=5 -)')
[%8 p=[%1 p=5] q=[%0 p=2]]
```

Since +make assumes no subject, all information must be provided in the expression. Furthermore, although not present explicitly, +make utilizes an internal $type of %noun.

```
> (make '-')
[%0 p=2]

> .*([1 2] (make '-'))
1
```

Text→AST→Nock. The simplified high-level lifecycle of Hoon code sees it go from text to an abstract syntax tree (AST) and thence to executable Nock.[5]

To convert Hoon text from a cord to an AST, use +ream. The AST is a tree of Hoon expressions marked by rune and components such as wings (lookup names in the subject) and atoms or cells.

```
> (ream '(add 1 2)')
[%cncl p=[%wing p=~[%add]] q=~[[%sand p=%ud q=1]
                                [%sand p=%ud q=2]]]

> (ream '-:!>(5)')
[%tsgl p=[%cnts p=~[[%.y p=2]] q=~]
                q=[%zpgr p=[%sand p=%ud q=5]]]
```

A Hoon AST is properly a $hoon, which is a complicated type union over all of the kinds of things that Hoon knows something to be able to be.[6] Sugar runes can be represented simply or reparsed by +open:ap into a more fundamental form. However, at this point no desugaring has taken place; equivalent forms may still have different AST representations as $hoon:

[5] In practice, the text is commonly derived from a file via the %hoon mark.

[6] The relevant code may be found in /sys/hoon.

```
> (ream '~[1 2 3]')
[%clsg p=~[[%sand p=%ud q=1] [%sand p=%ud q=2]
  [%sand p=%ud q=3]]]

> (ream '[1 2 3 ~]')
[%cltr p=~[[%sand p=%ud q=1] [%sand p=%ud q=2]
  [%sand p=%ud q=3] [%bust p=%null]]]
```

Hoon supplements "pure" values with metadata to establish context for the values and enforce its notion of type.

Given a reduced Hoon AST, `+mint:ut` function compiles it into Nock code. `+mint:ut` parses from a Hoon AST into a pair of the type and the Nock.[7]

```
> (~(mint ut %noun) %noun (ream '~[1 2 3]'))
[#t/[@ud @ud @ud %~] q=[%1 p=[1 2 3 0]]]
```

While there is much to say about `+mint`, for our purposes we simply note that it operates on each tag in an AST to convert it recursively to `$nock`.[8]

3 Vases

A `$vase` is a pair of `$type` and value, where `$type` defines the Hoon type set and the tail contains the actual data. (Vases could be treated more generally than simply Hoon types, but in practice are used only with Hoon, so the type data structure will become relevant.)

Vases received bare mention in the 2016 Urbit whitepaper (`~sorreg-namtyv` et al., 2016). They were noted merely as having the property of allowing a statically typed compiler to operate on dynamically typed runtime code—and thus, to reload portions of the kernel from source while running.

[7] One simple approach to understand this part of the Hoon compiler backend is to look at the 2013 Hoon compiler, which presents a relatively uncluttered version.

[8] Nock code is not executed simply in either of the primary runtimes, Vere or NockVM (f/k/a Sword, née Ares). Instead it is converted into a bytecode for execution.

However, vases are critically important to practical code composition and execution on Urbit and NockApp as functional-as-in-paradigm execution environments:

> Everything about a scope, including name bindings, aliases, and docstrings, is stored in the subject's type. This allows Hoon's compilation discipline to be similarly minimal: the compiler is a function from subject type and Hoon source to product type and compiled Nock. Running this Nock against a value of the subject type produces a vase of the result. It's hard to imagine a more streamlined formalism for compilation. (`~rovyns-ricfer`, 2019)

That is, vases enable the end developer to work at a higher level of abstraction than raw typed code and data would itself make straightforward in a statically typed functional programming environment.

Hoon's type information captures both the set of nouns valid for a particular piece of data and the subject, or environment to which the value has access. For instance, a `%face` is a lookup index into the subject for a value with an associated name.

Vases are frequently used to compile and execute Hoon code, but are also used to store typed data. Since Nock is ultimately homoiconic, any arbitrary noun may be either executable code or static data. A vase preserves the type information associated with the noun, making it possible to reconstruct it in regular (static) Hoon. For instance, as a security mechanism, "live code" is never transmitted over the wire between machines. Instead, the type and value are sent, and the recipient compiles the noun into executable code.

What vases permit over raw Nock manipulations therefore includes:

1. allowing types to be straightforwardly combined
2. permitting code evaluation (Lisp `eval`)
3. facilitating metacircular interpretation

4. managing persistent code artifacts

5. building and running system upgrades while running live (i.e. hotswapping code)

Urbit's application architecture has a persistent solid-state kernel which runs user applications in a sort of sandbox. They cannot use vase mode directly, but they are built and modified using vase mode. In particular, library imports and the REPL interface both use vase mode extensively.

Likewise, NockApp supplies a kernel wrapping specialized I/O drivers for the executable Nock, produced by Hoon or Jock. Vases are generally used for building code sent as nouns over the wire and in the compilers.

3.1 Hoon Type

The formal definitions of `$vase` and `$type` are as follows:

```
+$  vase  [p=type q=*]
+$  type  $~  %noun
          $@  $?  %noun
                  %void
              ==
          $%  [%atom p=term q=(unit @)]
              [%cell p=type q=type]
              [%core p=type q=coil]
              [%face p=$@(term tune) q=type]
              [%fork p=(set type)]
              [%hint p=(pair type note) q=type]
              [%hold p=type q=hoon]
          ==
```

- `%noun` is the superset of all nouns.
- `%void` is the empty noun, but won't occur in results (i.e. a compiler affordance).
- `%atom` spans the set of all atoms.
- `%cell` contains ordered pairs.

The other types are more complex:

- `%core` is the descriptor type for a core. Besides the `$type`, it uses a `$coil`, which is a tuple of variance information, context, and chapters (limbs).
- `%face` spans the same set as nouns but includes a face.
- `%fork` is a union, or choice over options.
- `%hint` is an annotation for the compiler (Nock opcode 11).
- `%hold` types are lazily evaluated, such as a recursive type (like the `+list` mold builder).
  - `%hold` types are why the compiler can have trouble with lists at runtime, such as needing to distinguish a `lest` or the TMI problem with `+snag` &c.
  - A `%hold` type is a "finite subtype" of an infinite type. Hoon doesn't actually know about these directly, just in that it can be lazy about evaluating recursions.
  - They result from arms in cores because the `hoon` of the arm is played against the core type as the subject type to get the result. This permits polymorphism, since the core can be modified to have a sample of a different type.

> One can "evaluate" a hold by asking the compiler to "play" the hoon against the subject type, meaning to infer what type of value would result from running that hoon against a value of the subject type. For a recursive type, this result type refers to the same hold, usually in one or more of the cases of a `%fork`. (`~rovnys-ricfer`, personal communication)

For instance, let's evaluate a value of the type `(list @ud)` using Hoon:

```
> =a `(list @ud)`~[1 2 3]

> !>(a)
[#t/it(@ud) q=[1 2 3 0]]

> -<:!>(a)
%hold

> -<:!>(?~(a 0 a))
%fork

> ->-:!>(?~(a 0 a))
#t/@ud
[%atom p=%ud q=~]

> ->+<:!>(?~(a 0 a))
l=[#t/[i=@ud t=it(@ud)] l=~ r=~]
```

(As an aside, while `+vase` is a reasonable name for a thing and the thing that shapes it, the original term was `+vise`, which also works in this capacity.)

3.2 Producing Vases

While vases can be constructed manually, Hoon provides several affordances for producing vases that are less error-prone and more convenient.

The most common way to produce a vase is to use the `!>` zapmic rune. This takes a noun and produces a vase of the raw value and its type.

```
> !>(~[1 2 3])
[#t/[@ud @ud @ud %~] q=[1 2 3 0]]
```

Note that the type is very literal: in this case, it is a three-tuple rather than a list. Hoon's type inference is quite literalistic, and this commonly leads to the "too much information" (TMI) problem, in which the type is too specific to be useful.

In Nock, we are essentially pinning a new variable at the head of our existing formula, then our tail is the actual access by binary tree address.

```
> %+  ~(mint ut %noun)
    %noun
  (ream '=/(a 5 =/(b 10 [a b]))')
[@ @]
[8 [1 5] 8 [1 10] [[0 6] [0 2]]]
```

Now, we may have values which appear identical in their resultant Nock, but which Hoon would enforce different type constraints upon, such as a null-terminated tuple of finite length and a list:

```
:: null-terminated tuple
> (compile (ream '~[1 2 3]'))
[#t/[@ud @ud @ud %~] q=[%1 p=[1 2 3 0]]]

:: formal list type with deferred evaluation
> (~(mint ut -:!>(.)) %noun (ream '(gulf 1 3)'))
[#t/it(@) q=[%8 p=[%9 p=200.245.085 q=[%0 p=1.023]]
 q=[%9 p=2 q=[%10 p=[p=6 q=[p=[%7 p=[%0 p=3]
 q=[%1 p=1]] q=[%7 p=[%0 p=3] q=[%1 p=3]]]]
 q=[%0 p=2]]]]]
```

We have to be able to envase and devase a value, which we will write Lisp-style. We also want to be able to combine vases by "slopping" them together. Finally, we need to "slap" an expression we wish to evaluate against a vase. Everything else in vase mode can be built out of these primitives.

> A vase is a pair of type and data, particularly as used in Nock and related languages. Vase mode, therefore, describes working with such pairs rather than first-order typed data. The vase algebra allows types to be straightforwardly combined, permitting code evaluation, facilitating metacircular interpretation, managing persistent code artifacts, and otherwise working at a higher level of abstraction than raw typed code and data. In this talk, we will examine the role of vases, the vase algebra, and work through several examples of how and why vase mode is useful throughout Nock-based platforms.

We employ two main tools in Hoon to envase (or make dynamic) and devase (or make static):

- `!>` zapgar envases, producing a vase from a noun.
- `!<` zapgal devases, producing a noun from a vase.

There is also a "typed quote" `!;` zapmic rune, which wraps the product of its second child as the type of the example given as the first child. This is not commonly used.

```
> !;  *type  [1 0x0]
[#t/[@ud @ux] 1 0x0]
```

3.3 Eliminating Vases

`!<` zapgal devases, which requires you to know what type you expect so that you can match them. This process is less common; while you can trivially ascend from a statically-typed environment to a dynamically-typed one, to enter Hoon's static layer again is more difficult and you have to know exactly what the type of the result is beforehand. (If the value does not fit the type it claims, we say that it is an "evil vase" and cannot process it.) Normally, once you have a vase in the code builder, you will use the vase algebra which we will discuss in a moment to produce static untyped Nock code instead of static Hoon code.

(A quick review of the Urbit kernel code base suggests that most instances of `!<` zapgal unsafe vase elimination are either unpacking command-line arguments which have in principle been vetted by the runtime first, or handling a received value over the network, presumably from its remote counterpart.)

4 Vase Algebra[9]

The essential operators on vases are `+slop` and `+slap`. Essentially all other operations can be expressed in terms of these two, but many supplemental operators are supplied with the Hoon compiler for convenience.

[9]This section benefitted from discussions with `~rovnys-ricfer`, to whom I am indebted.

4.1 `+slop`

If one queries the Hoon REPL what the vase of a pair of numbers is, it generates the following description:

```
> !>([100 200])
[#t/[@ud @ud] q=[100 200]]

> !<([@ud @ud] !>([100 200]))
[100 200]
```

Let's suppose that one intends to append a hexadecimal number as a tail. The original vase no longer holds:

```
> !>([[100 200] 0x12c])
[#t/[[@ud @ud] @ux] q=[[100 200] 300]]

> !<([[@ud @ud] @ux] !>([[100 200] 0x12c]))
[[100 200] 0x12c]
```

Combining these manually can be done, but it's rather tedious and error-prone in general. To combine them dynamically one can use the first tool of our vase algebra, `+slop`. `+slop` combines two vases, which means combining their types and their values consistently.

Here, `+slop` produces the cell of those two nouns:

```
> !>([100 200])
[#t/[@ud @ud] q=[100 200]]

> !>(0x12c)
[#t/@ux q=300]

> (slop !>([100 200]) !>(300))
[#t/[[@ud @ud] @ud] q=[[100 200] 300]]
```

`+slop` simply combines heads and tails using a `%cell` head tag:

```
++  slop
  |=  [hed=vase tal=vase]
  ^-  vase
  [[%cell p.hed p.tal] [q.hed q.tal]]
```

4.2 `+slap`

Chief among our list of reasons to use vases was the ability to dynamically evaluate code at runtime. How do we actually write code to `+slap` a given Hoon expression against a subject as vase? The `+slap` operator is the second part of the vase algebra. It takes a Hoon expression and a vase, and produces a new vase of the computational result.

```
++  slap
  |=  [vax=vase gen=hoon]  ^-  vase
  =+  gun=(~(mint ut p.vax) %noun gen)
  [p.gun .*(q.vax q.gun)]
```

With that, we can resolve a variable name (or "face") against a vase:

```
> !>(a=42)
[#t/a=@ud q=42]

> (slap !>(a=42) (ream 'a'))
[#t/@ud q=42]

> (slap !>(a=42) (ream '[a a]'))
[#t/[@ud @ud] q=[42 42]]
```

A much more interesting case arises when we introduce functions to the mix. Since we always need to know about a function to evaluate it, we will henceforth `+slop` in the Hoon subject including its standard library as `.` dot. Furthermore, if we don't have variable names in this example, we can refer to the values by their binary tree addresses, in this case the head of the tail and the tail of the tail.

```
> (slap (slop !>([a=1 b=2]) !>(.)) (ream '(add a b)'))
[#t/@ q=3]

> (slap (slop !>([1 2]) !>(.)) (ream '(add +6 +7)'))
[#t/@ q=3]
```

(It is conventional to `+slop` new information to the head of the subject because of the binary tree search order.)

4.3 Supplemental Operators

What else would we like to be able to do, given a subject?

The received wisdom from core developers has been that one can build whichever higher-level operations one needs from `+slap` and `+slop`. This seems to be more or less true, but the mechanics of it start to depend very much on your high-level language and its relation to the instruction set architecture it targets. In practice, Hoon provides some supplemental functions for vase mode because we need to handle the stack trace for errors as well as supplying a context for certain out-of-subject references in userspace code.

1. `+slam` is an affordance for easy execution of a Hoon gate or function. Given a gate and its arguments as vases, produce a vase containing the result.

```
> (slam !>(|=([a=@ud b=@ud] [b a])) !>([1 2]))
[#t/[@ud @ud] q=[2 1]]
```

2. `+slym` is an untyped version of `+slam`. The type of the sample (argument) is ignored, and the type of the resulting vase is determined by the gate alone. This is particularly useful with the "wet" gate system, which is a paradigm of gate-building gates used frequently in Hoon. Coming from a higher-level typed language, there is more than one way to build a Nock gate. Hoon, for instance, uses what are called "dry" and "wet" approaches. (In Jock, all gates are dry.)
   Put briefly, a dry gate is essentially a regularly typed gate: function argument types are checked and then inserted into the AST expression, which is built via vases in the conventional way.

   In contrast, a wet gate is more like a C-style macro, in which the types are accepted as tentatively passing the necessary checks, then as long as they work the original types are passed back out as appropriate. It's a way of asking if the Nock formula itself will just work—if it will, then build it and return the associated type we expect. (This is how typed lists are built, for instance.)

You see wet gates used frequently as gate builders—that is, if you need a gate operating for a particular type, the easiest way to do it is to produce a gate specialized by type. (You can see the dynamism enabled by vases shining through the cracks of this model.)

3. `+slab` tells us, given a subject, whether a name is present.

```
> (slab %read %a -:!>(a=5))
%.y

> (slab %read %a -:!>(b=5))
%.n
```

4. `+text` Vases are also used for the prettyprinter, since the conversion from raw value to standardized text output requires type information to resolve.

```
> (text !>(~[1 2 3]))
"[1 2 3 ~]"

> (text !>((gulf 1 3)))
"~[1 2 3]"
```

5. `+slew` retrieves the axis of a name in a vase.

6. `+swat` doubly defers a `+slap` operation for certain cases.

5 Applications of Vase Mode

5.1 Type Manipulation

Types can be manually constructed as necessary. For example, to manually reconstruct a `list` from a `lest` (or non-null `list`), we can use the `+slop` operator to combine a vase of the null terminator or empty list with the `lest`. (This is, of course, equivalent to upcasting back to a `list`, but the type system doesn't quite notice this directly as `it(@)`.) Because the collapse from dynamic vase mode to static Hoon code necessarily destroys some type information via the mold in `!<` zapgal, variants of this code work.

```
> =/  p  (gulf 1 5)
  !>(p)
[#t/it(@) q=[1 2 3 4 5 0]]

> =/  p  (gulf 1 5)
  ?~  p  !!
  !>(p)
[#t/[i=@ t=it(@)] q=[1 2 3 4 5 0]]

> =/  p  (gulf 1 5)
  ?~  p  !!
  (slop !>(~) !>(p))
[#t/[%~ i=@ t=it(@)] q=[0 1 2 3 4 5 0]]

> =/  p  (gulf 1 5)
  ?~  p  !!
  !<((lest @) (slop !>(~) !>(p)))
[i=0 t=~[1 2 3 4 5]]

> =/  p  (gulf 1 5)
  ?~  p  !!
  !<((list @) (slop !>(~) !>(p)))
~[0 1 2 3 4 5]
```

5.2 Code Evaluation

As a practical matter and a safety measure, executable Hoon code is not directly transmitted over the wire. Instead, the type and value are sent, and the recipient compiles the noun into executable code. This is a security measure to prevent arbitrary code execution.

Thus vases are used in the kernel and in userspace for certain kinds of transmitted code and data operations, including pokes between user agents. In fact, `~rovnys-ricfer` has produced a minimal working example of a userspace handler using vase mode.[10]

5.3 Metacircular Interpretation

Nock is a crash-only language; it has no error handling when run raw. To produce a manageable system, Nock is almost always run in a virtualized mode called `+mock`. While the main operator of this engine works only on raw untyped Nock, some of the adjuncts do preserve type for subsequent use of the outputs as statically-typed values to be raised back into vases at various points in the compiler. By providing a `$roof` or reference overlay to the fake Nock 12 opcode, for instance, a Nock runtime can supply a referentially transparent expedient even when the perceptual subject is much more constrained.

5.4 Persistent Code Artifacts

Urbit's Arvo kernel and Vere runtime, as well as the NockApp framework with the Sword runtime, aggressively cache vases to expedite code execution. Vases are stored in a map from their hash to the vase itself. This is a performance optimization, since the type information is expensive to compute and the value is expensive to reduce. For instance, Arvo's `$worm` cache maps Hoon vases to pairs of type and Nock nouns.

5.5 System Upgrades

A solid-state Nock runtime such as Arvo consists of an event loop over a list of input events to apply to a current state. System upgrades such as kernel updates are supplied and built using vases.

A meta-vase is a `vase` of a `vase`, that is, an untyped `vase`. These can be used to check structural data nesting without enforcing type, for instance. (Urbit types used to be total; that is, on a mismatch they would return their default rather than crashing.)

---

[10] See his video of ~2022.5.10; at the time of press, a copy is available at `https://drive.google.com/file/d/10SaE5doCfdeqc2j945t8GvGvexKIBBZq/view`.

The vane interface is normally strictly typed, but using a metavase it can punch a hole through the `type` system. (Before `!<` zapgal was introduced, vase reduction was mediated by a vane passing to the Arvo kernel to get into double vase mode, which Arvo would collapse into one vase mode and hand back.)

Since Urbit is built to handle hot-swapped kernel updating, one interesting complication with vase handling lies in upgrades to the type system itself:

> Some subtleties regarding types arise when handling OTA updates, since they can potentially alter the type system. Put more concretely, the type of type may be updated. In that case, the update is an untyped Nock formula from the perspective of the old kernel, but ordinary typed Hoon code from the perspective of the new kernel. Besides this one detail, the only functionality of the Arvo kernel proper that is untyped are its interactions with the Unix runtime.

A Nock runtime can cache known vases aggressively for performance improvement.

6 Beyond the Vase Algebra

Hoon used to directly expose many of the mechanics of this when file handles could be produced using a sophisticated but complicated build system.[11] While Hoon still uses vase mode explicitly to import libraries and deliver user agent pokes, these are the only places that a userspace developer would typically encounter them. The vase algebra has largely been restricted to the compiler level in contemporary practice.

6.1 Comparisons

Pairing type and data is a general and generalizable approach. Languages and compilers must, after all, track typed values in some way. How do other languages and systems handle this?

[11] To wit, the history of the Ford vane, ca. 2016–2019.

6.1.1 Python/CPython

For instance, in the CPython reference implementation all values are "boxed", or `PyObject` structures. This pairing of metadata and value is similar to the way that Hoon vases work, but it is not directly exposed as a first-class element of the Python user environment, nor is there an explicit vase algebra (or subject).

6.1.2 Assembly Language

Typed assembly languages such as TAL (Morrisett et al., 1999) were explored in the late 1990s and early 2000s, with the goal of providing a type-safe assembly language that could be used to write low-level code while still preserving type safety. These researchers recognized that traditional compilation procedures often destroyed type information when it was still useful for verification and optimization. Even dependently typed assembly languages have been explored (Xi and Harper, 2001), conceived as a way of improving bytecode or assembly level performance by permitting the compiler more optimizations than it would naively know enough to implement. A set of rules was defined in order to produce well-formed "type states", or relationships of type index expressions to actual register contents. This approach offers the expedient of a certifying compiler designed to guarantee type safety. While not constituting a vase algebra, the process of retaining type to produce better target ISA code shares a goal with Hoon's vase mode.

6.1.3 Lisp Quote

In Lisp, `'` is used to defer evaluation, or to treat an expression as data which can be introspected and evaluated at will.

```
(+ 1 2)              ; => 3
'(+ 1 2)             ; => (+ 1 2)
```

Without `'`, `(+ 1 2)` evaluates to 3. With `'`, it's a list or S-expression:

```
(list '+ '1 '2)
```

This is very similar to the way that Hoon lets you directly construct and manipulate an AST, as with +ream.

```
(define prog '(+ 1 2))
(car prog)          ; => +
(cdr prog)          ; => (1 2)
(eval prog)         ; => 3

(eval '(+ 1 2))   ; => 3
```

This is basically equivalent to Hoon's +ream, although the Hoon AST is somewhat more regularized and opaque.

```
> (ream '(add 1 2)')
[%cncl p=[%wing p=~[%add]] q=[i=[%sand p=%ud q=1]
  t=[i=[%sand p=%ud q=2] t=~]]]

> !,(*hoon (add 1 2))
[%cncl p=[%wing p=~[%add]] q=[i=[%sand p=%ud q=1]
  t=[i=[%sand p=%ud q=2] t=~]]]
```

A vase is a typed value that an AST, like ' or +ream produces, can be evaluated against. Lisp uses a global or explicit environment, whereas Hoon always lets you supply a subject of your choice, including the "current" subject (with .).

Vase mode is thus a "typed dynamic" system, unlike Lisp's raw dynamism. (Why not just use eval? Scheme is untyped and error-prone here. Vases add type safety, which in Hoon's case is used to delimit possible kinds of operations.)

6.1.4 Haskell Dynamic

Haskellers probably immediately think of Dynamic, which is used for injecting values into a dynamically typed value. Dynamic lets you pack values of different types into a uniform container and defer type checking until runtime. Like Hoon's vase mode, Dynamic lets you escape static typing temporarily and deferring type resolution. Whereas in Hoon, a type–value mismatch is an "evil vase" and results in a runtime crash,[12] Dynamic will result in Nothing if the types don't match.

[12]Since we are commonly running in an emulated mode, this doesn't take down the whole kernel.

Hoon's vases are in a sense much closer to the metal since they can trivially result in Nock code. Vase mode feels more like a dynamic interpreter or a VM, while `Dynamic` is more focused on typed payloads for data evaluation.

6.1.5 Untyped Virtual Machines

There may even be reason to eschew vases altogether in some cases; Jock does not currently use vases except when interacting with Hoon via a foreign function interface. Chevalier-Boisvert (2022) argued that untyped virtual machines are more resistant to bit rot than typed virtual machines:

> An untyped VM design ... has to enforce a small set of hard constraints, such as making sure that pointer dereferences respect valid address bounds so that the running program can't crash the host VM, but it doesn't really need to care about the types of values or enforcing typing constraints. For performance, it can implement a very barebones JIT compiler based on dynamic binary translation, but it doesn't have to care about optimizing type checks, and it can even allow the running program to manage its own memory and implement its own garbage collector.
>
> ... [T]here's a strong case to be made that an untyped VM design can easily be much smaller and more minimalistic than a typed VM design. A simpler untyped VM has two major strengths. The first is that it doesn't place as many restrictions on running programs. Programs can implement their own control flow structures, their own GC, or even their own JIT. The second is that a smaller, simpler VM is much easier to port, reimplement and maintain. (Chevalier-Boisvert, 2022)

Nock runtimes do indeed hew to this parsimony, but vases are used particularly in interprocess communication in today's Urbit kernel and userspace. It is unclear how they could profitably be excised from the system given their global utility.

A final interesting question is to think about targeting other ISAs. While Hoon itself is closely tied to Nock, no part of the vase algebra (in the abstract) is specific to Nock except its instantiation as nouns.

7 Conclusion

Vase mode provides something like a gradual (un)typing pipeline: one proceeds from a static Hoon context, to a dynamic vase mode, to untyped Nock. A vase algebra describes how to combine the type subject information and the associated value information, as in an import or a REPL. This lets Hoon have human-legible affordances in metaprogramming and validation, while retaining a simple target ISA for execution, code proving, and optimized execution.

References

Chevalier-Boisvert, Maxime (2022) "Typed vs. Untyped Virtual Machines". URL: `https://pointersgonewild.com/2022/06/08/typed-vs-untyped-virtual-machines/` (visited on ~2024.7.4).

Morrisett, Greg et al. (1999). "TALx86: A Realistic Typed Assembly Language." In: *Proceedings of the 1999 ACM SIGPLAN Workshop on Compiler Support for System Software.* ACM, pp. 25–35. URL: `https://www.cs.cornell.edu/talc/papers/talx86-wcsss.pdf` (visited on ~2024.7.4).

`~rovyns-ricfer`, Ted Blackman (2019) "Why Hoon?" URL: `https://urbit.org/blog/why-hoon` (visited on ~2025.8.13).

`~sorreg-namtyv`, Curtis Yarvin et al. (2016). *Urbit: A Solid-State Interpreter.* Whitepaper. Tlon Corporation. URL: `https://media.urbit.org/whitepaper.pdf` (visited on ~2024.1.25).

Xi, Hongwei and Robert Harper (2001). "A Dependently Typed Assembly Language." In: *Proceedings of the 6th ACM SIGPLAN International Conference on Functional Programming (ICFP'01)*. ACM, pp. 169–180.

A Documentary History of the Nock Combinator Calculus

N. E. Davis ~lagrev-nocfep,
Curtis Yarvin ~sorreg-namtyv
Zorp Corp, Urban Tiger

Abstract

Nock is a family of computational languages derived from the SKI combinator calculus. It serves as the ISA specification layer for the Urbit and NockApp systems. This article outlines the extant historical versions of the Nock combinator calculus and reconstructs the motivation for the changes made at each kelvin decrement. It begins with an exposition of Nock as a tool of computation, outlines the history of Nock's decrements, and speculates on motivations for possible future developments.

Contents

Urbit Systems Technical Journal II:2 (2025): 155–190.
Address author correspondence to ~lagrev-nocfep.

1 Introduction

Nock is a combinator calculus which serves as the computational specification layer for the Urbit and Nockchain/NockApp systems. It is a hyper-RISC instruction set architecture (ISA) intended for execution by a virtual machine (but see `~mopfel-winrux`, pp. 99–130 in this volume). Nock's simplicity and unity of expression make it amenable to proof-based reasoning and guarantees of correctness. Its Lisp-like nature surfaces the ability to introspect on the code itself, a property which higher-level languages compiling to it can exploit. Yet for all this, Nock was not born from a purely mathematical approach, but found its roots in practical systems engineering.

Nock permits itself a finite number of specification changes, called "decrements" or "kelvins", which allow it to converge on a balance of expressiveness and efficacy. This article outlines the extant historical versions of the Nock combinator calculus and reconstructs the motivation for the changes made at each kelvin decrement. It begins with an exposition of Nock as a tool of computation, outlines the history of Nock's decrements, and speculates on motivations for possible future developments.

2 Nock as a Combinator Calculus

Fundamental computer science research has identified a family of universal computers which may be instantiated in a variety of ways, such as the Turing machine, the lambda calculus, and the combinator calculus. Equivalence theorems such as the Church–Turing thesis show that these systems are equivalent in their computational power, and that they can be used to compute any computable function. The combinator calculus is a family of systems which use a small set of combinators to express computation. The most well-known member of this family is the SKI combinator calculus, which uses only three combinators: S, K, and I. Other members of this family include the BCKW combinator calculus and the H combinator calculus. These systems are all equivalent in their computational power, but they differ in their syntax and semantics. The Nock combinator calculus is an extension of the SKI combinator calculus which adds a few axiomatic rules to navigate and manipulate binary trees, carry out a very primitive arithmetic, and provide for side effects.

Put perhaps better, Nock is a family of combinator calculi that sequentially converge on an "optimal" expressiveness for certain design desiderata. This includes an economy of expression (thus several macro opcodes) and consideration of how a higher-level language would invoke stored procedural expressions. Furthermore an opcode exists which produces and then ignores a computation, intended to signal to a runtime layer that a side effect may be desired by the caller.[1]

Nock bears the following characteristics:

- Turing-complete. Put formally, Turing completeness (and thus the ability to evaluate anything we would call a computation) is exemplified by the μ-recursive functions. In practice, these amount to operations for constant, increment, variable access, program concatenation, and looping (Reitzig, 2012). Nock supports these directly through its primitive opcodes.

[1]An able if dated document from January 2010, `5-whynock.txt`, further expounds desiderata for Nock in the context of Urbit as operating function.

- Functional (as in language). Nock is a pure function of its arguments. In practice, the Urbit operating system provides a simulated global scope for userspace applications, but this virtualized environment reduces to garden-variety Nock. (See `~lacnes`, pp. 71–97 in this volume, for details of a Nock virtualized interpreter.)
- Subject-oriented. Nock evaluation consists of a formula as a noun to be evaluated against a subject as a noun. Taken together, these constitute the entire set of inputs to a pure function.

  Some Nock opcodes alter the subject (for instance a variable declaration) by producing a new subject which is utilized for subsequent axis lookups.
- Homoiconic. Nock unifies code and data under a single representation. A Nock atom is a natural number, and a Nock cell is a pair of nouns. Every Nock noun is acyclic, and every Nock expression is a binary tree. For example, Nock expressions intended to be evaluated as code are often pinned as data by the constant opcode until they are retrieved by evaluating the constant opcode at that axis.
- Untyped. Nock is untyped, meaning that it does not impose any type system on the expressions it evaluates. Nock "knows" about the natural numbers in two senses: such are used for addressing axes in the binary tree of a noun, and such are manipulated and compared using the increment and equality opcodes.
- Solid-state. A Nock interpreter is a solid-state machine, meaning that it operates from a state to a new state strictly according to inputs as a pure lifecycle function. The Nock interpreter must commit the results of a successful computation as the new state before subsequent computations, or events, can be evaluated. Transient evaluations (uncompleted events) and crashes (invalid evaluations) may be lost without consequence, and the

Nock interpreter layer persists the underlying state of the machine.

We have asserted without demonstration thus far that Nock is a combinator calculus. We now show that this is the case, with reference to Nock 4K, the latest specification. The simplest combinator calculus consists of only three combinators: S, K, and I (Wolfram, 2021). These combinators are:

1. S substitution. $\mathrm{S}xyz = xz(yz)$, returns the first argument applied to the third, then applies this to the result of the second argument applied to the third. This corresponds to Nock 4K's opcode 2, which substitutes the second argument into the first argument at the third argument's axis. (There are some subtle differences to Nock's expression of S as opcode 2 that we will elide as being fundamentally similar, but perhaps worthy of its own monograph.)

2. K constant. $\mathrm{K}xy = x$, consumes its argument and returns a constant in all cases. This corresponds to Nock 4K's opcode 1, which yields its argument as a constant noun.

3. I identity. $\mathrm{I}x = x$, returns its argument. This corresponds to a special case of Nock 4K's opcode 0, a generalized axis lookup operator, which can trivially retrieve the current subject or expression as well as any children.

While Nock introduces a few more primitive operations as a practicality, the above identities establish its bona fides as a combinator calculus capable of general computation. Similar to Haskell Curry's BCKW system, which can be written in forms isomorphic to SKI, Nock provides a set of primitive rules and a set of economic extended rules for convenience in writing a compiler.[2]

In an early document, Yarvin explained two of his design criteria in producing Nock as a practical ISA target (`~sorreg-namtyv`, 2010):

[2]See `~timluc-miptec`, pp. 1–45 in this volume, for exposition on how to evaluate a Nock expression by hand or by interpreter.

1. Natural conversion of source to code without other inputs.
2. Metacircularity without deep stacks; i.e., the ability to extend Nock semantics without altering the underlying substrate.

This latter idea he particularly connected to the concept of what came to be called a "scry namespace": "dereferencing Urbit paths is as natural (and stateless) a function as increment or equals" (ibid.). Indeed, Urbit's current userspace utilizes such an affordance to replicate a global scope environment for accessing system and remote resources. (See `~lacnes`, pp. 71–97 in this volume, for a discussion of the Nock virtualized interpreter.)

3 Nock's Decrements

The Nock family survives in a trail of breadcrumbs, with each version of the specification being a decrement of the previous version.[3] Early versions were produced exclusively by Curtis Yarvin, eventually involving the input of other developers after the 2013 founding of Tlon Corporation. In this section, we present each extant version of the Nock specification and comment on the changes and their motivations. Only the layouts have been changed for print. Dates for Nock specifications were derived from dated public posts (`U`, 9K), internal dating (13K, 12K, 11K, 10K), or from Git commit history data (8K, 7K, 6K, 5K).[4] No version of 14K survives publicly, nor does any primordial version prior to `U` (15K) appear to exist.

Yarvin's background as a systems engineer with systems like Xaos Tools (for SGI Irix), Geoworks (on DoCoMo's iMode), and Unwired Planet (on the Wireless Application Protocol, WAP) inclined him towards a formal break with Unix-era computing (`~sorreg-namtyv`, 2025). He sought to produce a sys-

[3] This system, called "kelvin decrementing", draws on analogy with absolute zero as the lowest possible temperature—and thus most stable state.

[4] In at least one case (7K), Yarvin claims to have finished the proposal a month earlier but to not have posted it until this date.

tem enabling server-like behavior rather than a network of clients dependent on centralized servers for a functional Internet. This required a deep first-principles rederivation of computing; the foundational layer was a combinator calculus which became Nock. Nock was intended from the beginning to become less provisional over time, encoding a kelvin decrement which forced the specification to converge on a sufficiently good set of opcodes. Many downstream consequences of Urbit and NockApp as systems derive directly from the affordances encoded into Nock.

3.1 U

> I have not really worked with combinator models, but my general impression is that it takes essentially an infinite amount of syntactic sugar to turn them into a programming language. `U` certainly takes some sweetener, but not, I think, as much. (`~sorreg-namtyv`[5], 2006)

The earliest extant Nock is `U`, a proto-Nock posted to the *Lambda the Ultimate* blog in 2006 (`~sorreg-namtyv` (2006); `~sorreg-namtyv` (2006)).[6] The draft is versioned 0.15; subsequent evidence indicates that this is a downward-counting kelvin-versioned document already. The full specification is reproduced in Listing 1.

Extensive commentary on the operators is provided. Rightwards grouping of tuple expressions has already been introduced. Extension of the language is summarily ruled out.[7] Data are conceived of as Unix-like byte streams; details of parsing and lexing are considered. Terms (the ancestor of nouns) include a `NULL`-like "foo" type ~ distinguishable by value rather than structure. ASCII is built in as numeric codes, evocative of Gödel numbering.

As commenter Mario B. pointed out, the `U` specification permits SKI operators with the simple expressions,

[5] *Avant la lettre*; synonymous with Curtis Yarvin throughout.

[6] Unfortunately many elements of the original prehistory of Nock appear to be lost to the sands of time on unrecoverable hard drives.

[7] Compare Ax and Conk by `~barpub-tarber`, pp. 191–228 in this volume.

```
[name]  [pattern]        [definition]
  (I)     (I $a)           $a
  (K)     (K $a $b)        $b
  (S)     (S $a $b $c)     ($a $c ($b $c))
```

While early work (1940s–50s) had been carried out on "minimal instruction set computers" (MISCs), it is more likely that Yarvin was influenced by contemporaneous work on "reduced instruction set computers" (RISCs) in the 1980s and 90s. Language proposals like that of Madore's Unlambda and Burger's Pico Lisp may have influenced Yarvin's design choices throughout this era.

The U specification is in some ways the single most interesting historical document of our series. Yarvin particularly identified a desire to avoid baking abstractions like variables and functions into the U cake, and an emphasis on client–server semantics. The scry namespace appears for the first time as a referentially transparent immutable distributed namespace. U expresses a very ambitious hyper-Turing operator, acknowledging that its own instantiation from the specification is impossible and approximate. Yarvin grapples in U with the halting problem (via his follow operator) and with the tension between a specification and an implementation (a gulf he highlighted as a human problem in his 2025 LambdaConf keynote address). Furthermore, asides on issues like the memory arena prefigure implementation details of Vere as a runtime.

Listing 1: U, 31 January 2006. The earliest extant patriarch of the Nock family.

```
U: Definition

1 Purpose
    This document defines the U function and its data
    model.

2 License
    U is in the public domain.

3 Status
    This text is a DRAFT (version 0.15).
```

4 Data

A value in U is called a "term." There are three kinds of term: "number," "pair," and "foo."

A number is any natural number (ie, nonnegative integer).

A pair is an ordered pair of any two terms.

There is only one foo.

5 Syntax

U is a computational model, not a programming language.

But a trivial ASCII syntax for terms is useful.

5.1 Trivial syntax: briefly

Numbers are in decimal. Pairs are in parentheses that nest to the right. Foo is "~".

Whitespace is space or newline. Line comments use "#".

5.2 Trivial syntax: exactly

```
term    : number
        | 40 ?white pair ?white 41
        | foo

number  : 48
        | [49-57] *[48-57]

pair    : term white term
        | term white pair

foo     : 126

white   : *(32 | 10 | (35 *[32-126] 10))
```

6 Semantics

U is a pure function from term to term.

This document completely defines U. There is no compatible way to extend or revise U.

6.1 Rules

```
[name]  [pattern]                [definition]

(a)     ($a 0 $b)                $b
(b)     ($a 1 $b $c)             1
(c)     ($a 1 $b)                0
(d)     ($a 2 0 $b $c)           $b
(e)     ($a 2 %n $b $c)          $c
(f)     ($a 3 $b $c)             =($b $c)
(g)     ($a 4 %n)                +%n

(h)     ($a 5 (~ ~ $b) $c)       $b
(i)     ($a 5 (~ $b $c) $d)      *($a $b $c $d)
(j)     ($a 5 (~ ~) $b)          ~
(k)     ($a 5 (~ $b) $c)         *($a $b $c)
(l)     ($a 5 ($b $c) $d)
                    (*($a $b $d) *($a $c $d))
(m)     ($a 5 $b $c)             $b

(n)     ($a 6 $b $c)    *($a *($a 5 $b $c))
(o)     ($a 7 $b)                *($a 5 $a $a $b)
(p)     ($a 8 $b $c $d)          >($b $c $d)

(q)     ($a $b $c)      *($a 5 *($a 7 $b) $c)
(r)     ($a $b)                  *($a $b)
(s)     $a                       *$a
```

The rule notation is a pseudocode, only used in this file. Its definition follows.

6.2 Rule pseudocode: briefly

Each line is a pattern match. "%" means "number." Match in order. See operators below.

6.3 Rule pseudocode: exactly

Both pattern and definition use the same evaluation language, an extension of the trivial syntax.

An evaluation is a tree in which each node is a term, a term-valued variable, or a unary operation.

Variables are symbols marked with a constraint. A variable "$name" matches any term. "%name" matches any number.

There are four unary prefix operators, each of which is a pure function from term to term: "=", "+", "*", and ">". Their semantics follow.

6.4 Evaluation semantics

For any term $term, to compute U($term):

- find the first pattern, in order, that matches $term.
- substitute its variable matches into its definition.
- compute the substituted definition.

Iff this sequence of steps terminates, U($term) "completes." Otherwise it "chokes."

Evaluation is strict: incorrect completion is a bug. Choking is U's only error or exception mechanism.

6.5 Simple operators: equal, increment, evaluate

=($a $b) is 0 if $a and $b are equal; 1 if they are not.

+%n is %n plus 1.

*$a is U($a).

6.6 The follow operator

>($a $b $c) is always 0. But it does not always complete.

We say "$c follows $b in $a" iff, for every $term:

```
if *($a 5 $b $term) chokes:
    *($a 5 $c $term) chokes.

if *($a 5 $b $term) completes:
    either:
        *($a 5 $c $term) completes, and
        *($a 5 $c $term) equals
          *($a 5 $b $term)
    or:
        *($a 5 $c $term) chokes.
```

If $c follows $b in $a, >($a $b $c) is 0.

If this statement cannot be shown (ie, if there exists any $term that falsifies it, generates an infinitely recursive series of follow tests, or is inversely self-dependent, ie, exhibits Russell's paradox), >($a $b $c) chokes.

7 Implementation issues

This section is not normative.

7.1 The follow operator

Of course, no algorithm can completely implement the follow operator. So no program can completely implement U.

But this does not stop us from stating the correctness of a partial implementation - for example, one that assumes a hardcoded set of follow cases, and fails when it would otherwise have to compute a follow case outside this set.

U calls this a "trust failure." One way to standardize trust failures would be to standardize a fixed set of follow cases as part of the definition of U. However, this is equivalent to standardizing a fixed trusted code base. The problems with this approach are well-known.

A better design for U implementations is to depend on a voluntary, unstandardized failure mechanism. Because all computers have bounded memory, and it is impractical to standardize a fixed memory size and allocation strategy, every real computing environment has such a mechanism.

For example, packet loss in an unreliable packet protocol, such as UDP, is a voluntary failure mechanism.

If the packet transfer function of a stateful UDP server is defined in terms of U, failure to compute means dropping a packet. If the server has no other I/O, its semantics are completely defined by its initial state and packet function.

7.2 Other unstandardized implementation details
A practical implementation of U will detect and log common cases of choking. It will also need a timeout or some other unspecified mechanism to abort undetected infinite loops.

(Although trust failure, allocation failure or timeout, and choke detection all depend on what is presumably a single voluntary failure mechanism, they are orthogonal and should not be confused.)

Also, because U is so abstract, differences in implementation strategy can result in performance disparities which are almost arbitrarily extreme. The difficulty of standardizing performance is well-known.

No magic bullet can stop these unstandardized issues from becoming practical causes of lock-in and incompatibility. Systems which depend on U must manage them at every layer.

Source: ~sorreg-namtyv (2006).

3.2 Nock 13K

At some point between January 2006 and March 2008, Nock acquired its cognomen.

The only compound opcode is opcode 6, the conditional branch opcode.

Axiomatic operator * tar[8] is identified as a GOTO.[9]

Listing 2: Nock 13K, 8 March 2008.

```
Author: Curtis Yarvin (curtis.yarvin@gmail.com)
Date: 3/8/2008
Version: 0.13

1. Manifest

    This file defines one Turing-complete function,
    "nock."

    nock is in the public domain.  So far as I know,
    it is neither patentable nor patented.  Use it at
    your own risk.

2. Data

    Both the domain and range of nock are "nouns."

    A "noun" is either an "atom" or a "cell."  An
    "atom" is an unsigned integer of any size.  A
    "cell" is an ordered pair of any two nouns, the
    "head" and "tail."

3. Pseudocode

    nock is defined in a pattern-matching pseudocode.

    Match precedence is top-down.  Operators are
```

[8]We refer to Nock axiomatic operators via their modern aural ASCII pronunciations. While these evolved over time (to wit, ^ "hat" became "ket"), to attempt to synchronize pronunciation with the era of a Nock release is a fool's errand.

[9]One can see the influence of this version's naming scheme on ~barpub-tarber's Ax, pp. 191–228 in this volume.

```
    prefix.  Parens denote cells, and group right:
    (a b c) is (a (b c)).

4. Definition

4.1 Transformations

      *(a 0 b c)    =>  *(*(a b) c)
      *(a 0 b)      =>  /(b a)
      *(a 1 b)      =>  (b)
      *(a 2 b)      =>  **(a b)
      *(a 3 b)      =>  &*(a b)
      *(a 4 b)      =>  ^*(a b)
      *(a 5 b)      =>  =*(a b)
      *(a 6 b c d)  =>  *(a 2 (0 1)
                              2 (1 c d) (1 0)
                              2 (1 2 3) (1 0) 4 4 b)
      *(a b c)      =>  (*(a b) *(a c))
      *(a)          =>  *(a)

4.2 Operators

4.2.1 Goto (*)

      *(a)                -> nock(a)

4.2.2 Deep (&)

      &(a b)              -> 0
      &(a)                -> 1

4.2.3 Bump (^)

      ^(a b)              -> ^(a b)
      ^(a)                -> a + 1

4.2.4 Same (=)

      =(a a)              -> 0
      =(a b)              -> 1
      =(a)                -> =(a)
```

```
4.2.5 Snip (/)

    /(1 a)              -> a
    /(2 a b)            -> a
    /(3 a b)            -> b
    /((a + a) b)        -> /(2 /(a b))
    /((a + a + 1) b)    -> /(3 /(a b))
    /(a)                -> /(a)
```

Source: ~sorreg-namtyv (2008d).

3.3 Nock 12K

Opcodes were reordered slightly. Compound opcodes were introduced, such as a conditional branch and a static hint opcode. Autocons appeared explicitly.

Listing 3: Nock 12K, 2008.

```
Author: Curtis Yarvin (curtis.yarvin@gmail.com)
Date: 3/28/2008
Version: 0.12

1. Introduction

    This file defines one function, "nock."

    nock is in the public domain.

2. Data

    A "noun" is either an "atom" or a "cell."  An
    "atom" is an unsigned integer of any size.  A
    "cell" is an ordered pair of any two nouns,
    the "head" and "tail."

3. Semantics

    nock maps one noun to another.  It doesn't
    always terminate.

4. Pseudocode
```

```
     nock is defined in a pattern-matching
     pseudocode, below.

     Parentheses enclose cells.  (a b c) is
     (a (b c)).

5. Definition

5.1 Transformations

      *(a (b c) d) => (*(a b c) *(a d))
      *(a 0 b)     => /(b a)
      *(a 1 b)     => (b)
      *(a 2 b c)   => *(*(a b) c)
      *(a 3 b)     => **(a b)
      *(a 4 b)     => &*(a b)
      *(a 5 b)     => ^*(a b)
      *(a 6 b)     => =*(a b)

      *(a 7 b c d) => *(a 3 (0 1) 3 (1 c d) (1 0)
                          3 (1 2 3) (1 0) 5 5 b)
      *(a 8 b c)   => *(a 2 (((1 0) b) c) 0 3)
      *(a 9 b c)   => *(a c)

      *(a)         => *(a)

5.2 Operators

5.2.1 Goto (*)

      *(a)               -> nock(a)

5.2.2 Deep (&)

      &(a b)             -> 0
      &(a)               -> 1

5.2.4 Bump (^)

      ^(a b)             -> ^(a b)
      ^(a)               -> a + 1
```

```
5.2.5 Same (=)

      =(a a)            -> 0
      =(a b)            -> 1
      =(a)              -> =(a)

5.2.6 Snip (/)

      /(1 a)            -> a
      /(2 a b)          -> a
      /(3 a b)          -> b
      /((a + a) b)      -> /(2 /(a b))
      /((a + a + 1) b)  -> /(3 /(a b))
      /(a)              -> /(a)
```

Source: ~sorreg-namtyv (2008c).

3.4 Nock 11K

Opcodes were reordered slightly. The conditional branch was moved to 2. Composition, formerly at 2, was removed.

The kelvin versioning system here became explicit (rather than implicitly decreasing minor versions).

Listing 4: Nock 11K, 25 May 2008.

```
Author: Mencius Moldbug (moldbug@gmail.com)
Date: 5/25/2008
Version: 11K

1. Introduction

    This file defines one function, "nock."

    nock is in the public domain.

2. Data

    A "noun" is either an "atom" or a "cell."  An
    "atom" is an unsigned integer of any size.  A
    "cell" is an ordered pair of any two nouns, the
    "head" and "tail."
```

3. Semantics

nock maps one noun to another. It doesn't always terminate.

4. Pseudocode

nock is defined in a pattern-matching pseudocode, below.

Parentheses enclose cells. (a b c) is (a (b c)).

5. Definition

5.1 Transformations

```
*(a (b c) d) => (*(a b c) *(a d))
*(a 0 b)     => /(b a)
*(a 1 b)     => (b)
*(a 2 b c d) => *(a 3 (0 1) 3 (1 c d) (1 0)
                   3 (1 2 3) (1 0) 5 5 b)
*(a 3 b)     => **(a b)
*(a 4 b)     => &*(a b)
*(a 5 b)     => ^*(a b)
*(a 6 b)     => =*(a b)

*(a 7 b c)   => *(a 3 (((1 0) b) c) 1 0 3)
*(a 8 b c)   => *(a c)

*(a)         => *(a)
```

5.2 Operators

5.2.1 Goto (*)

```
*(a)            -> nock(a)
```

5.2.2 Deep (&)

```
&(a b)          -> 0
&(a)            -> 1
```

```
5.2.4 Bump (^)

          ^(a b)              -> ^(a b)
          ^(a)                -> a + 1

5.2.5 Same (=)

          =(a a)              -> 0
          =(a b)              -> 1
          =(a)                -> =(a)

5.2.6 Snip (/)

          /(1 a)              -> a
          /(2 a b)            -> a
          /(3 a b)            -> b
          /((a + a) b)        -> /(2 /(a b))
          /((a + a + 1) b)    -> /(3 /(a b))
          /(a)                -> /(a)
```

Source: ~sorreg-namtyv (2008b).

3.5 Nock 10K

Parentheses were replaced by brackets. Opcodes were reordered slightly. Hint syntax was removed. Functionally, 11K and 10K appear very similar, particularly if the Watt (proto-Hoon) compiler is set up to produce variable declarations and compositions as the compound opcodes had them.

Listing 5: Nock 10K, 15 September 2008.

```
Author: Mencius Moldbug [moldbug@gmail.com]
Date: 9/15/2008
Version: 10K

1. Introduction

  This file defines one function, "nock."

  nock is in the public domain.

```

2. Data

A "noun" is either an "atom" or a "cell." An "atom" is an unsigned integer of any size. A "cell" is an ordered pair of any two nouns, the "head" and "tail."

3. Semantics

nock maps one noun to another. It doesn't always terminate.

4. Pseudocode

nock is defined in a pattern-matching pseudocode, below.

Brackets enclose cells. [a b c] is [a [b c]].

5. Definition

5.1 Transformations

```
*[a [b c] d] => [*[a b c] *[a d]]
*[a 0 b]     => /[b a]
*[a 1 b]     => [b]
*[a 2 b c d] => *[a 3 [0 1] 3 [1 c d]
                    [1 0] 3 [1 2 3] [1 0] 5 5 b]
*[a 3 b]     => **[a b]
*[a 4 b]     => &*[a b]
*[a 5 b]     => ^*[a b]
*[a 6 b]     => =*[a b]
*[a]         => *[a]
```

5.2 Operators

5.2.1 Goto [*]

```
*[a]           -> nock[a]
```

5.2.2 Deep [&]

```
    &[a b]              -> 0
    &[a]                -> 1

5.2.4 Bump [^]

    ^[a b]              -> ^[a b]
    ^[a]                -> (a + 1)

5.2.5 Like [=]

    =[a a]              -> 0
    =[a b]              -> 1
    =[a]                -> =[a]

5.2.6 Snip [/]

    /[1 a]              -> a
    /[2 a b]            -> a
    /[3 a b]            -> b
    /[(a + a) b]        -> /[2 /[a b]]
    /[(a + a + 1) b]    -> /[3 /[a b]]
    /[a]                -> /[a]
```

Source: ~sorreg-namtyv (2008a).

3.6 Nock 9K

The cell detection axiomatic operator underlying opcode 4 (cell detection) was changed from & pam to ? wut. Versus 10K, 9K elides operator names in favor of definitions. Other differences are likewise primarily terminological, such as the replacement of Deep & pam with ? wut.

This version of Nock was published on the Moron Lab blog in 2010 (~sorreg-namtyv, 2010) as "Maxwell's equations of software". Yarvin emphasized that Nock was intended to serve as "foundational system software rather than foundational metamathematics" (ibid.). Yarvin also publicly expounded on the practicality of building a higher-level language on top of Nock at this point (ibid.):

> To define a language with Nock, construct two

nouns, `q` and `r`, such that `*[q r]` equals `r`, and `*[s *[p r]]` is a useful functional language. In this description,

- `p` is the function source;
- `q` is your language definition, as source;
- `r` is your language definition, as data;
- `s` is the input data.

More concretely, Watt (the predecessor to Hoon, ~sorreg-namtyv (2010)) is defined as:

```
urbit-formula == Watt(urbit-source)
              == Nock(urbit-source watt-formula)
watt-formula == Watt(watt-source)
             == Nock(watt-source watt-formula)
```

This remains the essential pattern followed to this day by higher-level languages targeting Nock as an ISA.

Yarvin had prepared to virtualize Nock interpretation to expose a broader namespace for interaction with values than the "strict" subject of a formula (~sorreg-namtyv, 2010).

Listing 6: Nock 9K, *terminus ad quem* 7 January 2010.

```
1 Context

    This spec defines one function, Nock.

2 Structures

    A noun is an atom or a cell.  An atom is any
    unsigned integer.  A cell is an ordered pair of
    any two nouns.

3 Pseudocode

    Brackets enclose cells.  [a b c] is [a [b c]].

    *a is Nock(a).  Reductions match top-down.

4 Reductions
```

```
?[a b]             => 0
?a                 => 1

^[a b]             => ^[a b]
^a                 => (a + 1)

=[a a]             => 0
=[a b]             => 1
=a                 => =a

/[1 a]             => a
/[2 a b]           => a
/[3 a b]           => b
/[(a + a) b]       => /[2 /[a b]]
/[(a + a + 1) b]   => /[3 /[a b]]
/a                 => /a

*[a 0 b]           => /[b a]
*[a 1 b]           => b
*[a 2 b c d]       => *[a 3 [0 1] 3 [1 c d] [1 0]
                        3 [1 2 3] [1 0] 5 5 b]
*[a 3 b]           => **[a b]
*[a 4 b]           => ?*[a b]
*[a 5 b]           => ^*[a b]
*[a 6 b]           => =*[a b]
*[a [b c] d]       => [*[a b c] *[a d]]
*a                 => *a
```

Source: ~sorreg-namtyv (2010c).

3.7 Nock 8K

The compound opcodes reappeared. Opcode 6 defined a conditional branch. Opcode 7 was described as a function composition operator. Opcode 8 served to define variables. Opcode 9 defined a calling convention. The remaining opcodes are hints, but each serving a different purpose:

11. consolidate for reference equality.

12. yield an arbitrary, unspecified hint.

13. label for acceleration (jet).

Nock 8K received an uncharacteristic amount of commentary, given a preprint document prepared for presentation at the 42nd ISCIE International Symposium on Stochastic Systems Theory and Its Applications (SSS'10) (`~sorreg-namtyv`, 2010).

Lambda was highlighted as a design pattern (a "gate" or stored procedure call) enabled by the "core" convention. Notably, `[[sample context] battery]` occurred in a different order than has been conventional since 2013 (emphasizing that the ubiquitous core pattern is a convention rather than a requirement). Watt was revealed to have a different ASCII pronunciation convention than Nock at this stage.

Listing 7: Nock 8K, 25 July 2010.

```
1 Structures

    A noun is an atom or a cell.  An atom is any
    unsigned integer.  A cell is an ordered pair of
    nouns.

2 Pseudocode

    [a b c] is [a [b c]]; *a is nock(a).  Reductions
    match top-down.

3 Reductions

    ?[a b]              0
    ?a                  1
    ^a                  (a + 1)
    =[a a]              0
    =[a b]              1

    /[1 a]              a
    /[2 a b]            a
    /[3 a b]            b
    /[(a + a) b]        /[2 /[a b]]
    /[(a + a + 1) b]    /[3 /[a b]]

    *[a [b c] d]        [*[a b c] *[a d]]
```

```
*[a 0 b]          /[b a]
*[a 1 b]          b
*[a 2 b c]        *[*[a b] *[a c]]
*[a 3 b]          ?*[a b]
*[a 4 b]          ^*[a b]
*[a 5 b]          =*[a b]

*[a 6 b c d]      *[a 2 [0 1] 2 [1 c d] [1 0]
                    2 [1 2 3] [1 0] 4 4 b]
*[a 7 b c]        *[a 2 b 1 c]
*[a 8 b c]        *[a 7 [7 b [0 1]] c]
*[a 9 b c]        *[a 8 b 2 [[7 [0 3] d] [0 5]]
                                             0 5]
*[a 10 b c]       *[a 8 b 8 [7 [0 3] c] 0 2]
*[a 11 b c]       *[a 8 b 7 [0 3] c]
*[a 12 b c]       *[a [1 0] 1 c]

^[a b]            ^[a b]
=a                =a
/a                /a
*a                *a
```

Source: ~sorreg-namtyv (2010b).

3.8 Nock 7K

During this era, substantial development took place on the early Urbit operating system. Nock began to be battle-tested in a way it had not previously been stressed. Several decrements occurred in short order.

The three hint opcodes were refactored into two, a static and a dynamic hint, both at 10.

Listing 8: Nock 7K, *terminus ad quem* 14 November 2010.

```
1 Structures

  A noun is an atom or a cell.  An atom is any
  natural number.  A cell is any ordered pair of
  nouns.

2 Pseudocode
```

```
[a b c]              [a [b c]]
nock(a)              *a

?[a b]               0
?a                   1
^a                   1 + a
=[a a]               0
=[a b]               1

/[1 a]               a
/[2 a b]             a
/[3 a b]             b
/[(a + a) b]         /[2 /[a b]]
/[(a + a + 1) b]     /[3 /[a b]]

*[a [b c] d]         [*[a b c] *[a d]]

*[a 0 b]             /[b a]
*[a 1 b]             b
*[a 2 b c]           *[*[a b] *[a c]]
*[a 3 b]             ?*[a b]
*[a 4 b]             ^*[a b]
*[a 5 b]             =*[a b]

*[a 6 b c d]         *[a 2 [0 1] 2 [1 c d] [1 0]
                         2 [1 2 3] [1 0] 4 4 b]
*[a 7 b c]           *[a 2 b 1 c]
*[a 8 b c]           *[a 7 [[7 [0 1] b] 0 1] c]
*[a 9 b c]           *[a 7 c 0 b]
*[a 10 b c]          *[a c]
*[a 10 [b c] d]      *[a 8 c 7 [0 3] d]

^[a b]               ^[a b]
=a                   =a
/a                   /a
*a                   *a
```

Source: ~sorreg-namtyv (2010a).

3.9 Nock 6K

The axiomatic operator for increment was changed from ^ ket to + lus. Compound opcode syntax was reworked slightly.

Listing 9: Nock 6K, 6 July 2011.

```
1 Structures

  A noun is an atom or a cell.  An atom is any
  natural number. A cell is an ordered pair of
  nouns.

2 Reductions

  nock(a)             *a
  [a b c]             [a [b c]]

  ?[a b]              0
  ?a                  1
  +a                  1 + a
  =[a a]              0
  =[a b]              1

  /[1 a]              a
  /[2 a b]            a
  /[3 a b]            b
  /[(a + a) b]        /[2 /[a b]]
  /[(a + a + 1) b]    /[3 /[a b]]

  *[a [b c] d]        [*[a b c] *[a d]]

  *[a 0 b]            /[b a]
  *[a 1 b]            b
  *[a 2 b c]          *[*[a b] *[a c]]
  *[a 3 b]            ?*[a b]
  *[a 4 b]            +*[a b]
  *[a 5 b]            =*[a b]

  *[a 6 b c d]        *[a 2 [0 1] 2 [1 c d] [1 0]
                                2 [1 2 3] [1 0] 4 4 b]
  *[a 7 b c]          *[a 2 b 1 c]
  *[a 8 b c]          *[a 7 [[0 1] b] c]
```

```
*[a 9 b c]           *[a 7 c 0 b]
*[a 10 b c]          *[a c]
*[a 10 [b c] d]      *[a 8 c 7 [0 2] d]

+[a b]               +[a b]
=a                   =a
/a                   /a
*a                   *a
```

Source: ~sorreg-namtyv (2011).

3.10 Nock 5K

Compound opcode syntax was reworked slightly. All trivial reductions of axiomatic operators were removed to the preface of the specification.

(For instance, a trivial "cosmetic" change was made to 5K's specification after it was publicly posted in order to synchronize it with the VM's behavior (dd779c1).)

Listing 10: Nock 5K, 24 September 2012.

```
1 Structures

  A noun is an atom or a cell.  An atom is any natural
  number.  A cell is an ordered pair of nouns.

2 Reductions

  nock(a)             *a
  [a b c]             [a [b c]]

  ?[a b]              0
  ?a                  1
  +[a b]              +[a b]
  +a                  1 + a
  =[a a]              0
  =[a b]              1
  =a                  =a

  /[1 a]              a
  /[2 a b]            a
```

```
/[3 a b]              b
/[(a + a) b]          /[2 /[a b]]
/[(a + a + 1) b]      /[3 /[a b]]
/a                    /a

*[a [b c] d]          [*[a b c] *[a d]]

*[a 0 b]              /[b a]
*[a 1 b]              b
*[a 2 b c]            *[*[a b] *[a c]]
*[a 3 b]              ?*[a b]
*[a 4 b]              +*[a b]
*[a 5 b]              =*[a b]

*[a 6 b c d]          *[a 2 [0 1] 2 [1 c d] [1 0] 2
                                    [1 2 3] [1 0] 4 4 b]
*[a 7 b c]            *[a 2 b 1 c]
*[a 8 b c]            *[a 7 [[7 [0 1] b] 0 1] c]
*[a 9 b c]            *[a 7 c 2 [0 1] 0 b]
*[a 10 [b c] d]       *[a 8 c 7 [0 3] d]
*[a 10 b c]           *[a c]

*a                    *a
```

Source: ~sorreg-namtyv (2012).

3.11 Nock 4K

The primary change motivating 5K to 4K was the introduction of an edit operator # hax, which ameliorated the proliferation of cells in the Vere runtime's memory.[10] The edit operator is an optimization which makes modifications to a Nock data structure more efficient. It's a notable example of a change motivated by the pragmatics of the runtime rather than theoretical or higher-level language concerns.[11] As ~fodwyt-ragful, one of the chief architects of this change, explained,

[10]The dating of 4K is diffuse, deriving from discussions and tests throughout 2018. It must be considered earlier than 27 September 2018; cf. urbit/urbit #1027.

[11]See ~niblyx-malnus, pp. 47–70 in this volume, for a verbose derivation of the edit operator and opcode 10 from the primitive opcodes.

> It carries the intent better than the equivalent autocons, which can (and does, in Vere's case) carry into implementation. Vere's edit operation checks if the target of the edit is 1) on the current road and 2) has a refcount of 1, and if so it does the edit in-place – meaning, it mutates the memory rather than consing up a new object. (Personal communication)[12]

Opcode 5 (equality) was rewritten to be more explicit with application of the cell distribution rule—in particular, `[5 0 1]` was valid in Nock 5K but difficult to optimize for in a practical compiler. Opcodes 6–9 were rewritten to utilize the * tar operator rather than routing via opcode 2. Opcode 11 (formerly opcode 10) was likewise massaged. In general, preferring to express rules using * tar proved to be slightly more terse than utilizing opcode 2.

Listing 11: Nock 4K, *terminus ad quem* 27 September 2018.

```
Nock 4K

A noun is an atom or a cell.  An atom is a natural
number.  A cell is an ordered pair of nouns.

Reduce by the first matching pattern; variables match
any noun.

nock(a)             *a
[a b c]             [a [b c]]

?[a b]              0
?a                  1
```

[12]Furthermore, `~fodwyt-ragful` clarified how these changes related to his work on the Nock bytecode interpreter. "The relationship between the bytecode interpreter and the changes in 4K is only circumstantial. For instance, one of the things I did while working on the bytecode was implement `edit` and benchmark it against the version without `edit`. We could see that we got an improvement, and that was going on at the same time the changes were being considered [anyway]. It would be inaccurate to say that something about the process of writing a bytecode interpreter caused us to realize that an `edit` operator in Nock would be a good idea" (Personal communication).

```
+[a b]              +[a b]
+a                  1 + a
=[a a]              0
=[a b]              1

/[1 a]              a
/[2 a b]            a
/[3 a b]            b
/[(a + a) b]        /[2 /[a b]]
/[(a + a + 1) b]    /[3 /[a b]]
/a                  /a

#[1 a b]            a
#[(a + a) b c]      #[a [b /[(a + a + 1) c]] c]
#[(a + a + 1) b c]  #[a [/[(a + a) c] b] c]
#a                  #a

*[a [b c] d]        [*[a b c] *[a d]]

*[a 0 b]            /[b a]
*[a 1 b]            b
*[a 2 b c]          *[*[a b] *[a c]]
*[a 3 b]            ?*[a b]
*[a 4 b]            +*[a b]
*[a 5 b c]          =[*[a b] *[a c]]

*[a 6 b c d]      *[a *[[c d] 0 *[[2 3] 0 *[a 4 4 b]]]]
*[a 7 b c]          *[*[a b] c]
*[a 8 b c]          *[[*[a b] a] c]
*[a 9 b c]          *[*[a c] 2 [0 1] 0 b]
*[a 10 [b c] d]     #[b *[a c] *[a d]]

*[a 11 [b c] d]     *[[*[a c] *[a d]] 0 3]
*[a 11 b c]         *[a c]

*a                  *a
```

Source: ~sorreg-namtyv, ~rovnys-ricfer, & ~fodwyt-ragful (2018).

4 The Future of Nock

While deviations from the trunk line of the Nock family have been proposed at various points,[13] Nock itself has remained the definitional substrate of Urbit since its inception. It has also been adopted as the primary ISA of the NockApp ecosystem.

Why, then, do we contemplate further changes? The SKEW proposal spearheaded by `~little-ponnys` and `~siprel` (2020) argued that Nock 4K represented an undesirable saddle point in the design space of possible Nocks, itself a "ball of mud". While SKEW itself was not adopted, it inspired the development of Plunder and PLAN as a solid-state computing architecture sharing some ambitions with Urbit and Nock (Plunder, 2023). A rigorously æsthetic argument can thus be sustained that Nock is not yet "close enough" to its final, diamond-perfect form to be a viable candidate.

While some have found this argument compelling, Urbit's core developers have elected to maintain work in the main trunk of traditional Nock as the system's target ISA. The Nock 4K specification is a good candidate, in this sense, for a "final" version of Nock, as it has been successfully used in production for several years. It seems more likely that subsequent changes to Nock will derive not from alternative representations but from either dramatically more elegant expressions (e.g., of opcode 6 or a combinator refactor) or from an implicit underspecification in the current Nock 4K which should be made explicit.

5 Conclusion

> A13: If you don't completely understand your code and the semantics of all the code it depends on, your code is wrong.
>
> F1: If it's not deterministic, it isn't real.
>
> (`~wicdev-wisryt`, Urbit Precepts (2020))

[13]Notably, Ax (see `~barpub-tarber`'s Ax, pp. 191–228 in this volume), SKEW, and PLAN.

Nock began life as a hyper-Turing machine language, a theoretical construct for the purpose of defining higher-level programming languages with appropriate affordances and semantics. While its opcodes and syntax have gradually evolved over the course of two decades, the ambition to uproot the Unix "ball of mud" and replace it with a simple operating function amenable to reason has remained the north star of Urbit and Nock. The history of Nock serves as an index of refinement as Yarvin and contributors sought to balance conciseness, efficiency, and practicality.

The most recent version, Nock 4K, appears to provide all of the opcodes necessary for correct and efficient evaluation.[14] It is likely that future versions of Nock will be based genetically on Nock 4K, but with some changes to improve its performance and usability. The road to 0K is likely very long still, given an abundance of caution, but it also appears to be straight.

References

Burger, Alexander (2006) "Pico Lisp: A Radical Approach to Application Development". URL: `https://software-lab.de/radical.pdf` (visited on ~2025.5.19).

Madore, David (2003) "The Unlambda Programming Language". URL: `http://www.madore.org/~david/programs/unlambda/` (visited on ~2025.5.19).

Plunder (2023) "What is Plunder?" URL: `https://web.archive.org/web/20250422030425/https://plunder.tech/` (visited on ~2025.8.16).

Reitzig, Raphael (2012) "Are there minimum criteria for a programming language being Turing complete?" URL: `https://cs.stackexchange.com/questions/991/are-there-minimum-criteria-for-a-programming-language-being-turing-complete` (visited on ~2025.5.19).

[14]Modulo the vagaries of the von Neumann architecture, etc.

~sorreg-namtyv, Curtis Yarvin (2006a) "U, a small model". URL: http://lambda-the-ultimate.org/node/1269 (visited on ~2024.2.20).

— (2006b) "U, a small model". URL: http://urbit.sourceforge.net/u.txt (visited on ~2024.2.20).

— (2008a) "Nock 10K". URL: https://github.com/urbit/archaeology/blob/0b228203e665579848d30c763dda55bb107b0a34/Spec/nock/10.txt (visited on ~2024.2.20).

— (2008b) "Nock 11K". URL: https://github.com/urbit/archaeology/blob/0b228203e665579848d30c763dda55bb107b0a34/Spec/nock/11.txt (visited on ~2024.2.20).

— (2008c) "Nock 12K". URL: https://github.com/urbit/archaeology/blob/0b228203e665579848d30c763dda55bb107b0a34/Spec/nock/12.txt (visited on ~2024.2.20).

— (2008d) "Nock 13K". URL: https://github.com/urbit/archaeology/blob/0b228203e665579848d30c763dda55bb107b0a34/Spec/nock/13.txt (visited on ~2024.2.20).

— (2010a) "Nock 7K". URL: https://github.com/urbit/archaeology/blob/0b228203e665579848d30c763dda55bb107b0a34/Spec/nock/7.txt (visited on ~2024.2.20).

— (2010b) "Nock 8K". URL: https://github.com/urbit/archaeology/blob/0b228203e665579848d30c763dda55bb107b0a34/Spec/nock/8.txt (visited on ~2024.2.20).

— (2010c) "Nock 9K". URL: https://github.com/urbit/archaeology/blob/0b228203e665579848d30c763dda55bb107b0a34/Spec/nock/9.txt (visited on ~2024.2.20).

— (2010d) "Nock: Maxwell's equations of software". URL: http://moronlab.blogspot.com/2010/01/nock-maxwells-equations-of-software.html (visited on ~2024.1.25).

~sorreg-namtyv, Curtis Yarvin (2010e) "Urbit: functional programming from scratch". URL: http://moronlab.blogspot.com/2010/01/urbit-functional-programming-from.html (visited on ~2024.1.25).

— (2010f) "Watt: A Self-Sustaining Functional Language (preprint)". URL: https://github.com/cgyarvin/urbit/blob/master/Spec/watt/sss10.tex (visited on ~2025.5.19).

— (2010g) "Why Nock?" URL: https://github.com/cgyarvin/urbit/blob/gh-pages/Spec/urbit/5-whynock.txt (visited on ~2025.5.19).

— (2011) "Nock 6K". URL: https://github.com/urbit/archaeology/blob/0b228203e665579848d30c763dda55bb107b0a34/Spec/nock/6.txt (visited on ~2024.2.20).

— (2012) "Nock 5K". URL: https://github.com/urbit/archaeology/blob/0b228203e665579848d30c763dda55bb107b0a34/Spec/nock/5.txt (visited on ~2024.2.20).

— (2018) "Nock 4K". URL: https://docs.urbit.org/language/nock/reference/definition (visited on ~2024.2.20).

— (2025). "Urbit: Making the Future Real." In: *LambdaConf 2025*. Estes Park, Colorado: LambdaConf. URL: https://www.lambdaconf.us/ (visited on ~2025.5.19).

Wolfram, Stephen (2021). *Combinators: A Centennial View.* Champaign, Illinois: Wolfram Media. URL: https://www.wolfram.com/combinators/ (visited on ~2025.5.19).

Conk: The Permutation Group of Nocks
Ax: An Algebraic Executable Ur-Machine

Sam Atman ~barpub-tarber

Abstract

Conk, the permutation group of 720 Nock machines based on the ordering of primitive opcodes 0–5, is introduced. Ax is a specific cellular automaton for general purpose computation (a subclass disjoint by one member from Conk). First developed as a thought experiment on a Nock-like combinator calculus, Ax seeks to build a logical order of operators in sequence, starting from the definition of a noun. This historical document presents and explores Conk, Ax, and their ramifications for Nock-style combinator computing.

Contents

Urbit Systems Technical Journal II:2 (2025): 191–228.
Address author correspondence to ~barpub-tarber.

1 Conk: The Permutation Group of Nocks

There are 720 valid Nock machines, defined as any cellar automaton which provides a mapping from the Nock rewrite rules to any one of every digit of set `{0..5}`. Since one of them is actually called Nock, let's call the permutation group Conk.

Two of them are Ax machines, or would be, minus the `fz` operation. That is, there are two Conks which have the same mappings for `0`, `1`, `2`, and `3` [as the then-current Nock 5K]. There are actually six Ax machines, two of which have the same axioms as Nock machines; we may consider those two as Nock equivalent, by permuting `fz` above the Nock (proper) threshold of 10. By the same simple mathematics, there are 5,040 possible Conk-compliant machines computationally equivalent to Ax, Nock not among them. We will call this permutation group Xa.

Six is a small enough number to consider in entirety. The only bit that is arbitrary is the range on sigma σ, which is only arbitrary if you're not an extant silicon computer.

I am convinced Ax α is the best possible choice among the six. I hope to demonstrate that here.

There are an infinite number of cellular automata. Conk machines are a class. Ax machines are an interesting subclass, disjoint by one member.

2 Ax: An Algebraic Executable Ur-Machine

2.1 Specification

This text specifies Ax, a cellular automaton for general purpose computation. It is a work of mathematics in the public domain.

Preamble

1. A noun is either an atom or a cell. An atom is any natural number.

2. A cell is an ordered pair of nouns.

3. `n` refers to any atom. `a`, `b`, `c`, and `d` refer to nouns.

4. `Ξ` means to perform a rewrite as defined by this specification.

5. `→` shows the steps of such a reduction. All must be completed.

6. `?` means the reduction is undefined.

7. `:=` indicates a noun is the referent of a symbol.

8. `+` refers to the operation on the natural numbers, whose identity is `0`.

9. `~` requires that `n` so defined be in the range (`n1..n2`), inclusive.

10. `[a b c] → [a [b c]]`

11. Symbols have no other semantics.
12. The lemmas are reduced in ordinary arithmetic; `c` and `d` refer to atoms.

Term

```
~(0..1) := σ
```

Reduction

Axioms

```
Ξ [0]                  →  Ξ [0]
Ξ [0 0]                →  Ξ [0 0]
Ξ [0 0 0]              →   0
Ξ [0 1 0 0]            →   1
Ξ [0 1 0 1]            →   2
Ξ [2 1 2 1]            →   3
Ξ [a 0 b]              →   b
Ξ [a 1 0 n]            →   n + 1
Ξ [a 1 b]              →   Ξ [a b]   →    n    →    n + 1
Ξ [a 2 0]              →   ?
Ξ [a 2 1]              →   a
Ξ [[a b] 2 2]          →   a
Ξ [[a b] 2 3]          →   b
Ξ [a 2 (b + b)]        →    Ξ [Ξ [a 2 b] 2 2]
Ξ [a 2 (b + b + 1)]    →  Ξ [Ξ [a 2 b] 2 3]
Ξ [a 2 b]              →   Ξ [a 2 b]
Ξ [3 3 [[2 1] [1 2 1]] [0 2 1]]    →    [3 4]
Ξ [a [b c] d]          →  [Ξ [a b c] Ξ [a d]]
Ξ [a 3 b c]            →   Ξ [Ξ [a b] Ξ [a c]]
Ξ [a 4 b]              →   Ξ [a b]   →    [c c]    →   1
Ξ [a 4 b]              →   Ξ [a b]   →    [c d]    →   0
Ξ [a 5 b]              →   Ξ [[a σ] b]
Ξ [a 6 b]              →   Ξ [a b]   →    [c d]    →   1
Ξ [a 6 b]              →   Ξ [a b]   →      d      →   0
```

Expansion

Terms

```
7 operators                    7 lemmas

0  := is                       12 := dec
1  := inc                      13 := add
2  := br                       14 := sub
3  := ax                       15 := mul
4  := eq                       16 := div
5  := fz                       17 := mod
6  := cel                      18 := lt

5 idioms

7  := cmp
8  := if
9  := cnk
10 := put
11 := arm

Ξ [a 12 b]  →  Ξ [b [cnk [is 0]
  [cnk [is [if [eq [br 7] [up br 6]]
               [br 6]
               [arm 2 [[br 2] [up br 6] [br 7]]]]]
       [arm 2 br 1]]]]

etc.

Version 61K
```

2.2 Explanation

2.2.1 Axioms

Zero `0` is the identity operator, `is`. There are two operations that are closed over the monoid of the natural numbers, addition and multiplication. Of them, multiplication is consequent.

In the operation of addition, `0` returns the identity. If you have any number, you may now return it; you now have `0`:

```
Ξ [0 0 0] -> 0
```

One `1` is the increment operator, `up`, as premised in the preamble. If you have a number, and you now have `0`, you may increment it.

```
Ξ [0 0 1 0] -> 1
```

Two `2` is the branch operator, `branch`. You need `0`, `1`, `2` and `3` to define `branch`, but you can use `1` and `2` to produce `3`. `mod` being explicitly provided, we may write an expansion that actualy runs quite servicably. The Nock spec provides no way to factor `a` into `a + a`, nor to determine which of lines 15 or 16 to apply. This does not detract from its correctnesss, these are very ordinary operations on the natural numbers.

Branch *selects* a branch, it does not *cause* one. Branch/forking happens in the same two ways in Ax as in Nock, because Ax is a Nock machine. Note that `branch` on branch `0` (to apply `branch` is to 'graft' the subject and return a branch from it) is not a syntax error, but rather, undefined. It may be a syntax error if you wish, or produce a noun, which is a common anticipated use. It may even produce an effect, but that would be crazy. The spec doesn't say, though; grafting on zero means your code is not deterministic. Crashing is the best idea if you don't know what else to do.

Note that so far, we have halting rules and trivial crashes only. Next comes the distribution rule, which gets us most of the way there, and then the explicit recursion rule, `Ax`. These *cause* branches, and composing that ability with `branch` raises the bar.

How many operators does it take to write an infinite loop? I am curious, without the time to explore the question. I predict the set will be low ordered with respect to Ax. Consequently it will be composed of the operators `0..4`, inclusive, likely without `4`. We'll see.

Three 3 is the `ax` operator, `Ax`, which Nocks a noun apart and evals it. The symbol `nck` is also reserved for this operator, en homage.

Consider that there are two ways to index: by zero, and by one. What if you want to contain the damage? Well, you could count `(0|1) (1|2) (2|3) 4 5 6`, or `(0|1) (0|1) (2|3) (3|4) 4 5 6`. The latter is taxing on our already strained resources.

In certain circles this difficulty is referred to as the "Abyss". My solution to this difficulty is suggested by ancient texts but the interpretation is to my knowledge completely original. We are all fairly certain the mystery involves both `3` and `11`. Let's leave it at that for now.[1]

Note that both the distributive property and `Ax` may safely be made parallel once the cell to calculate both branches is composed. Indeterminate, mutually dependant behavior may be arranged only through abuse of the `0` branch and the `put` operator, in the usual fashion.

Four 4 is the `eq` operator, which returns `0` if the evaluated `cons(subject,object)` is equal and `1` if it is not, crashing on an atom.

Why is `4 eq`? Well, it's our first non-prime operator, if you accept the case that `0` and `1` are neither prime nor non prime. They have a special relationship with multiplication that makes that case plausible; certainly I was taught the primality of one, though the field would appear to have changed its mind.

It could be `cel`, but as we'll see, `cel` should not be 4. `eq`'s expansion may be thought of as having an 'even' test or a 'double even' test, that is, it `ifs` on `cel` (though of course, the reduction does not). If 'odd', test atomic equality, if 'even', apply `cel`. Note that all even-numbered operators and idioms have exactly two expansions, that is, they are higher order branching. Even `put` is capable of branching, depending on implementation.

Five 5 is the `fz` operator, one of the *raisons d'être* for Ax ver-

[1] `Ax` could be 2, but `branch` could not be 3, or we would have `[? 1 3 1]`, and where did that three come from? Also, branch on address 3 is not defined in the reductions.

sus Nock. Fully qualified Ax machines are not deterministic, because they aren't colorblind. In addition to Black and White bits, Ax machines must supply Red bits, which are completely different because they come from an actual, high-quality source of entropy. Note that, while weird, this is just as well formed as saying "an actual, high-quality source of numeric computations", in that you can just hop on the Internet and buy one. Ax machines must have both.

This is why `fz` must be an operator, not a lemma. The Second Law of Thermodynamics is taken as axiomatic for our purposes; within the specification, the method of selecting on the range is deliberately left unspecified.

The demonstration Ax machine uses Pink bits, which are only pseudorandom. This is strictly not compliant, for the purposes of a reference implementation, but I'm in a hurry. Feel free to use Pink bits if you're just futzing around, but consider making or buying a gig or two of entropy, or picking up an entropy machine. Cheap stuff, entropy, these days. Remember to throw it away as soon as you're done with it: the first rule of handling entropy is: any operation whatsoever upon it render it *and any copies* no longer entropic.

`5` has several expansions, for, among other reasons, compatibility with Hoon. Any Conk runs fine on a Xa, but for safety, we have an Ax rule that takes a `fz` result and `puts` it away, `is`ing a `0` instead, and then using the `0` to `is` the subject, turning it into a no-op. Anything `fz mul is 0` will return `0`, another convenient way of ignoring entropy. Lastly, one may expand `fz` by checking `branch 0` for `1` or `0`, discarding the result in the former case; this may easily be implemented as an on-off switch for an indeterminate function.

Lastly, note that randomness is not mentioned in the spec. It is actually perfectly valid for `fz` to return any number in the range: you may rewind Ax and play it again, or feed it nothing but `[1]` in all cases, or `0`, or anything else you'd like. The treatment of `5` and `branch 0` distinguishes the actual semantics of an Ax machine, as they introduce indeterminacy into the result.

Six 6 is the cell operator, `cel`. It returns `0` for a cell and `1` for an atom, as you might expect. Symbols are inspected in this case to see what kind of noun they represent.

Well, there are two important kinds of cells in Ax, `[a b]` and `[a b c]`, as defined in the preamble. There are two groupings of six, `[[1 1] [1 1] [1 1]]` and `[[1 1 1] [1 1 1]]`. If you immediately recognize those are syntax errors, you're doing great. Happily, Ax is blessed with exactly three relevant data structures, as shown by the first three lines of the reduction: atoms and two cells, which may not be Axed, and 3 cells, which are n cells, and which may be Axed in some cases.

Those are the axioms. I am totally convinced of `0`, `1`, `2`, and `3`, which define Ax space within Conk space. I am pretty sold on `4`, `5`, and `6`, and on the benefits of Xa space and the `a br 0` reduction of `2`.

Note that we may generate `6` with `Ξ [4 5 [2 3]]`. Eventually, or immediately, depending on the Ax machine. This is considered beneath demonstration.

The ordering of the idioms is basically Kabbalistic. That is the reasoning behind Ax space too. It happens to look like a Page from the Book, as Erdős Pál would say.

2.2.2 Idioms

Nock calls these macros, and defines them as such, though we are advised by the Crash Course[2] that there's no reason to implement them this way. In Ax we call them idioms, indicating that they may be expanded as macros containing only the axioms. For the reduction, sometimes we do, sometimes we don't, whatever's cleanest. Since we have expansion rewrites as well as reductions, anything may be written as a macro, as long as you're not in a hurry to halt.

`7` is `cmp`, which composes functions, and which, through happenstance, ended up in the same place as in Nock. We're in Netzach, if you're paying attention.

`8` is `if`, `9` is `cnk`, `10` is `put` and `11` is `arm`. `if`, `cnk` and `arm` work like `6`, `8`, and `9` from Nock, because they're identical except for

[2]Editor's note: The documentation at the time.

the necessary permutations. `put` has the same syntax as the other `10`, and identical semantics: the results are undefined, other than that evaluation must happen if a cell is provided. We don't plan on using this for hinting, but if we're running Hoon 191, what other option do we have?

`put` fits nicely in `10`, because it's `0` all over again, having the same meaning for the purposes of the Arc of code under evaluation. The interaction between `put` and `branch 0` is envisioned as a crucial mechanism in the larger Arcitecture.

I could make a firm case for `dec` as consonant to `inc` and `arm` as consonant to `branch`, giving an opposite mapping. But the lemmas come after the idioms, and `dec` is clearly a lemma, and that is that. Certainly, the Nock tutorial shows that `dec` may be (somewhat) compactly specified in terms of the axioms.

2.2.3 Lemmas

Ax comes equipped with the operations you'll need to have a reasonable Big *O* on integer algorithms.

2.3 Distinctions between Ax and Nock

There are four changes between Nock and Ax: the permutation of the operations, the addition of `fz`, `branch 0`, and the `put` operator, to list them in order of seriousness. I have made the case, I believe, that the permutations put the jewel in the heart of the lotus. Perhaps we merely gild the lily. This is a matter of taste, not semantics, but without taste, Nock is pointless. I have devoted a number of paragraphs to `fz` already. Let's discuss `branch 0` and `put`.

`branch 0` provides for a very simple and ordinary thing: a number that comes from Outside, that we can only determine if we go and look. A port, say, or a sensor. Nock does not explicitly handle such at all (a subject constructor must provide it to a formula). Ax does: you can hook a very simple piece of Ax up to a sensor and do things with the numbers. I consider this a virtue in a toy computer, and the zero branch was just sitting there being undefined.

I suggest a pleasant detour over to "Undefined Intimacy With the Machine" (Buswell, 2010). Not all code talks to Outside, but most code comes from Somewhere, and sometimes Somewhere might want to drop a noun or two into the mix. While this is what you do with Nock in practice, a runtime or operating context must provide it. The thing is that Ax machines make no assumption that the whole system is going to be running on one core, in fact they're decidedly more comfortable if that is not the case.

Could we run Ax machines on a ColorForth array? The Parallela is a less exotic target; if you know any OpenCL, the interaction between `branch 0` and `put` might be putting you in mind of a "kernel".

Why do we need `fz` though, with all this Undefined Intimacy going around? Well, because of the Rules of the Red Bit, basically. An undefined number is going to be some combination of Black and White when you look at it. A Red Bit is already Black or White, but it got that way in a very special manner, and you're not allowed to look at it (though you may copy it) or it's not Red anymore. Not to mention that sealed functions that use `fz` make perfect sense and should be allowed, and a function either crashes on `branch 0` or does something special with it, but not in general both.

`fz` is axiomatic, and we force you to write your code in weird ways if you absolutely want to be sure it never comes up. It's a feature! We call it guessing, and have this notion that it makes for cheap machine learning. We hope a group effort can come up with some good uses.

What about this `put` business? Well, we like the algebraic feature of Ax a lot. We don't need hints, because it's quite normal for Ax code to come with both embedded symbols and a table containing expansions for the symbols, as well as jets for the assisted ones. In a mature environment, we scrub this of any taint of variability and anonymize everything, so your `foo` and my `foo` will be different even if they happen to be equal (minus yet another layer of abstraction!). As it stands, AxUM is a single computation and all symbols must be distinct and have singular expansions.

We do have code with identical semantics, which seems like

an odd choice if we're forsaking hints. Here's one good reason: Ax goes to great lengths to be in principle Hoon and Nock compatible. It's just respectful, and if there's to be a transition, let's ease the pain, or delay it insofar as possible.

In fact, use of `put` will also not affect the semantics of your running code. If you're in some kind of compatibility mode, you may even find that the use of opcode `10` provides pleasant jet assistance to your calculations. This is not our intended use case: `put` is the other side of `branch 0`.

Without going into detail that will probably prove wrong, `branch 0` and `put` define address spaces "above" and "below" the Arc of Ax code that is executing. Nock is Hermetically sealed, which is a virtue; `branch 0` and `put` provide a formal, very low-level- mechanism for building plumbing between Ax vessels.

Getting this right will be the true test of the Tree of Life on this machine. The Tree is recursive, fractal, heirarchical, and mnemnonic, among other qualities, all of which comes into play.

Importantly, this is defined at a higher level. It will be the canonical way to link Ax machines together, but is not part of the semantics of the machines themselves, on purpose. They're really quite small.

The main reason for this is that the intricacy of these address spaces will make them in effect kernel-level abstractions. They will end up just as frozen as Ax will, but consequent to that, and with a longer annealing phase.

2.4 Philosophy

Well and good, and we all love an elegant mathematical structure. What's the purpose of some of this? Why an Ax machine, which is inductive, nondeterministic, and redundant, versus a Conk machine, which is crisp, deductive, and minimal?

It's not an idle question. There are two Conks with the elegance of the Ax machine, which are Ax α with operator 5 replaced with one of the two possible options. Why choose induction and expansion over deduction and reduction? Why even offer the choice? Usually, we choose computers that are known to halt on problems which are known to halt.

Well, Ax isn't quite that bad. It has a Ko rule, after all. There are two cases to be made, one from elegance and another from utility.

Without expansions, one may not generate the full set of possible operations from a seed. This is a beautiful property in a system, if you're me, and since the expansion `Ξ [0 0 0] -> Ξ [0 2 1]` may yield (I am convinced) the other operators, it is a beautiful seed for a beautiful system. This is sufficient justification for the automaton; what is mathematics if not elegance, nor elegance if not a species of beauty?

Utility is perhaps harder to see, but imagine an aging computer in a hostile environment. Though it has megas of cores, many are infected and firewalled, others punctured by radiation or otherwise deranged and useless. The ability to expand a failed reduction may save a calculation, and that's no minor thing. A failed or malfunctioning jet may be similarly unit tested against its expansion, fractally and repeatedly, and substitutes checked for correctness in the same way.

So that's the Ax machine. Maxwell's equations build each on the others, as Euclid's Axioms, as the Laws of Motion and Thermodynamics. With the Ax ordering of Nock, the operators produce their own sequence. Quod Erat Demonstrandum.

2.5 Comments on Ax

This historical document is excerpted for the portions most relevant to Ax's technical specification. The full document, including commentary on the philosophy of mathematics and computer science and an excursus on Hoon, is available at `https://github.com/mnemnion/ax/blob/master/comment.md`.

> Whence it is that the ultimate laws of Logic are mathematical in their form; why they are, except in a single point, identical with the general laws of Number; and why in that particular point they differ;—are questions upon which it might not be

> very remote from presumption to endeavour to pronounce a positive judgment. Probably they lie beyond the reach of our limited faculties. It may, perhaps, be permitted to the mind to attain a knowledge of the laws to which it is itself subject, without its being also given to it to understand their ground and origin, or even, except in a very limited degree, to comprehend their fitness for their end, as compared with other and conceivable systems of law. (George Boole, *An Investigation of the Laws of Thought*)

We concern ourselves today with this question: what is the most suitable representation for a computation? Does one such exist? If so, how would we know if we had found it?

I do not claim to have found it. That is a strong claim, here I make a weaker claim: that there is a property, which I will call consonance or sometimes clarity, that allows us to weakly order computing engines, and that by that property, Ax is the most consonant system of computation of which I am aware.

Ax extensively derives its formal structure from Nock. Nock is a formidable work of mathematics, put forth as a piece of system software; much as a caryatid may succeed both as art and as architecture, Nock succeeds in being both.

cgy (this is an honorific style in our culture) is suspicious of mathematics. This is an understandable error, but error it remains. We had the good fortune to be born just in time for the great wave of microprocessor technology to wash over our civilization. Part and parcel of this was that the really juicy, good and useful mathematics was done by engineers with graphite on their sleeves, slide rules, and great fanfold sheets of printed code.

This is not to denigrate the Bourbakis of the world. No doubt when things calm down a bit, we can sift through postwar mathematics looking for the nuggets of insight. They retreated into a private language, and I'm willing to grant that may have been necessary for their work. Will any of it ever have the impact on human civilization as, say, Dijkstra's pathfinding algorithm? I would wager it will not.

Dijkstra himself was emphatically a mathematician. Would we say the same of Ken Thompson and Rob Pike? Of course not, they are engineers. Yet the UTF-8 encoding is poised to be the very substance of human language for as long as our civilization lasts. The great work of unifying all systems of writing, undoing at least one small fraction of the disaster at Babel, or, if you prefer historicity to metaphor, succeeding for the first time in this great cause; if this is not mathematics, what then *is* mathematics? If you don't see a Page from the Book in the encoding diagram for UTF-8, dear Reader, venture elsewhere. You're not going to like the rest of this.

The actual encoding of Unicode onto bits and bytes is fairly good engineering, all things considered. Like all engineering, it is riddled with compromise, partial backwards compatibility, rancorous dispute, and all manner of path-dependent weirdness. (A glance at the Wiki will show the 6-byte UTF-8 is the true UTF-8; we are burdened with a paltry 21 bits of encoding for no good reason at all.) That this is a mistake, when designing a living standard with a one-way ratchet which admits mappings but cannot expel them, is a point I consider evident.

To return to our topic, Nock is presented as foundational system software, Urbit as an existence proof of its fitness to purpose. Very well, but EBCDIC was fit to IBM's purpose also. Is Nock an EBCDIC or is it the real-deal UTF-8?

Where the success of Urbit is concerned, cgy is a pig and I am a chicken. You see, one day the chicken said to the pig, "Let's open up a diner. We can call it Ham and Eggs". The pig said "Eh, I don't know about that. Sounds like you're just invested, but I'm committed". I wasn't the chicken in the anecdote, don't know which Tlön investor was, regardless, I have laid my egg, and received my Dukedom, in the form of the carrier[3] Emperor Constantine, now transformed into seat 12 on the Galactic Senate, all of which appeals to my roleplaying sensibilities. Curtis is all in; one senses he feels the fate of the world may rest on his shoulders, and who is to say it doesn't. He must either bring home the bacon, or become it.

---

[3] At an early stage in Urbit's Azimuth PKI, the metaphor for hierarchical points ran from carrier through cruisers, destroyers, yachts, to submarines.

I find myself in this peculiar position because I was promised Maxwell's Laws of Software, the firm foundation on which we may at last rest a computational edifice which actually makes sense (`~sorreg-namtyv`, 2010). The better comparison is to the Elements of Geometry, four axiomatic propositions which remain true, and one which remains good, thousands of years after their release into the wild.

Curtis finds himself here because he believes he has found them. I believe he came very close. A confession: until I actually visited Tlön in late 2013, I harbored a suspicion that Curtis had permuted the operators of Nock as a test.[4] At the time he was awarding Dukedoms as prizes for implementing decrement in Nock, and it seemed at least possible he was playing his cards close to the vest, to see if anyone else would notice. Perhaps he published a hash of the true Nock to a blockchain, as a reveal that he had priority.

This is still possible; due to the loobean nature of Nock (which reminds me of nothing so much as Pig Latin), and Ax's faithful attempt to remain compatible with it, the structure of Ax can perhaps admit of further improvement.[5] It's not the sense I'm getting, and I'll proceed as though Tlön in general considers Nock to admit no further improvement, and is building Urbit upon it on that basis. This is all complicated by the urgency a startup must feel to bring its product to market, and certainly I share their sense of mission. But the Laws of Software!

So I will make the case for Ax as clearly as I am able. I will make no great effort to separate that which Nock and Ax have in common from that which is distinct to Ax alone, though there will be the occasional discursion to discuss points of divergence. Anyone with the interest to examine them both will realize the great debt Ax owes Nock, and get a sense of the relative difficulty of the two achievements. Dig deeper, and you will find it's giants upon giants, all the way down.

---

[4]Editor's note: compare the alchemical practice of "fulminating gold".

[5]This realignment of Ax with the Boolean logic has been performed, and this decision is reflected in the rest of this document.

2.6 Ax

Ax is a computational automaton, based upon a formalism called a noun. Automaton, meaning its reductions are mechanical; we simply go down the list of reductions, in order, performing the first one we are able, and do this repeatedly until we either have a noun that admits no further reduction, or until we find ourselves in a trivial loop and grow weary, or until the Universe runs out of syntropy with which to drive the mechanics further. Whichever comes first.

It has a specification. What then of the genus, what is a computational automaton?

Computational because Ax exhibits a property called Turing completeness, meaning that in a certain important sense it is just as good as any other system with this property at performing all of the subset of mathematics called finite, or discrete. This is a useful subset, as it can be used through further abstraction to perform, or at least represent, any mathematical formalism at all. We now know that certain properties, particularly the logical consistency of those mappings in all cases, may not be proved; yet this fact has proven less devastating to the mathematical project than it first appeared.

Now, there are many automata which exhibit Turing completeness, a further result we call Turing equivalence. Properly speaking this means each of these systems may simulate any other, thus their power is in one important sense equivalent.

They are not in fact equal. Mathematical pranksters of a certain bent delight in designing esoteric Turing Machines which may be, with great difficulty, compelled to perform computations. This is great sport, but we don't use these machines for practical purposes, because they have a tendency to be slow, and are difficult to reason about by design. The latter is by far the greater flaw; as we will show, if we can reason about a slow computation, and be confident in our reasoning, we may often replace it with a fast one, and no one the wiser.

Another way in which they differ is in their danger to the user. Wouldn't you know it, Alan Turing again: these systems have a property called undecidability, meaning in principle, and often enough in practice, you must run a computation to achieve its result. Many machines in this class are all too easy to undermine, presenting by subterfuge a computation which appears to want one result, but which in fact produces quite another; the exposure of your private key, for example.

There is a simple automaton, which, as hackers are nothing if not whimsical, we commonly refer to through a vulgar combination of the organ of thought and act of generation. I will call it `T`, short for Turing Tape. `T` has an advantage over, say, the lambda calculus: it uses a flat array (the tape) containing a finite number of symbols, represented by natural numbers.

This last quality is important. From Shannon, we know that signal, at its most basic level, is either absent or present, and arrives in a specific order. These properties inexorably lead to a mapping between the natural numbers and the symbols so transmitted, brushing aside questions of endianness, word boundaries, encoding and the like. The lambda calculus leaves us with no obvious basis to send and receive it. `T` gives us a sharp nudge in the right direction.

There is a further and deeper virtue in the use of natural numbers to stand in for the elements of computation. This virtue, and its proper expression, are the primary concerns of this treatise. We will introduce this aspect in the next section, because we will need it before we reach the demonstrations and reductions of Ax.

The trouble with `T` is that flat tape. It means the distinction between data and code is not structural. While it is possible in principle to write an abstraction over flat data space which is not subject to subversion, in practice, any mistake however mere is likely to open up an avenue for pwnage.

This is part of why we use a noun. The encapsulation has properties which make mistakes harder, more local. What we receive from the network is always flat, and what we emit may as well be. Requiring that it be acted upon only if it is a noun, and only as a noun, gives us a first layer of sanity, and a structure upon which to impose the next.

Ax does this without detracting from the simplicity of `T`. We gain elegance, we don't lose it. While the formal power is equivalent, the expressive power is of a higher order. A reasonable `T` may be written with eight instructions; Ax has 19, of which it requires six or seven. I prefer to construe it in the latter sense, for reason I will discuss in section five. Let us call it optional; it is certainly opinionated.

2.6.1 On the Nature of Number

The nature of computation is elusive. It has its origin in calculation, an ancient series of discovered rules for working with numbers. What distinguishes computation from mere calculation?

The natural numbers have three cases, three essential senses in which they are meant. The first case is the cardinal case, which we learn from pebbles and blocks as children. When we count pebbles, we start with one. Calculation shares a root with chalk.

The second case is the ordinal case, where we say, "this is the first", second, and so on. Note that we use a different set of words here, but they are so strongly linked semantically as to seem like tenses of a single term, one and first, second and two, three and third. Only the last, and those that follow, track with their sounds the meaning of the cardinal.

Zero is the correct first. One, the correct second. Etc.

This was not evident, to put it mildly. In the Occident, until comparatively recent times, Zero was unknown as a cardinal quantity, as decimal representation was similarly unknown. Its place as the origin of the natural numbers was not fully elucidated until the nineteenth century, and the zero index remains a stumbling block for every student of computation. Who among us has not committed a fencepost error?

Zero's position as the first ordinal established, it has a cardinality also, denoting absence, but an absence which may be specific, as one may have no pebbles rather than nothing at all. This narrowing from Zero in the infinite to the original sense is evident from a glance at the hyperbolic graph. It is due to Zero's originality, that is, its use as the origin point of coordinate systems, that it was accepted as a natural number, and the prime ordinal.

The third case is the nominal. When boys go out afield, we put numbers on their backs to stand in for their names.

Little Jeremy is every bit as 27 as his hero, and there is joy in Mudville.

It is this nominal property with which we are typically concerned in a computation. Each character of this treatise is represented as a number, and while these were cleverly chosen they are as arbitrary as can be.

I think it is fair to say, also, that purpose distinguishes computation from calculation. We might sum either bushels of fruit grown or coins spent, wishing all the while that the first was larger and the second smaller. In general computation is done to a purpose, by or for a person, and calculation is the mechanical, or automatic, or algorithmic, aspect of a computation. This distinguishing quality we refer to as semantics, or meaning.

The Canaanites invented the connection between marks and phonemes; they used these same marks, in a style adopted wholesale by the Greeks, to represent number. This style included no mark for nullity or void, and this absence of absence leaves traces in our minds and tongues. Yet Zero is a most natural number, and it is the first.

The trick of computation is in the nominal case. Yet the natural numbers retain their virtues proper to their ordering, and their cardinal virtues also. If we are to enumerate reductions upon a noun, let us make these reductions consonant to those virtues. That which is prior must precede that which follows.

2.6.2 The Noun

```
A noun is either an atom or a cell.
An atom is any natural number.
A cell is an ordered pair of nouns.
```

This is the simplest possible data structure, which is also recursive. (This is how you know it is correct.) It is also acyclic, which is a good property to have.

2.6.3 Loops

```
Ξ [0]   →  Ξ [0]
Ξ [0 0]   →  Ξ [0 0]
```

These are the identity atom and the identity cell. Neither is reducible. Both loop endlessly on their own self. Pretty. But not calculation.

2.6.4 Identity

```
Ξ [0 0 0]          →   0
```

Zero has, as one of its cardinal properties, which are, again, those inherent to its being, the property of identity in addition. To add zero to any atom results in precisely that atom, neither more nor less.

Additionally, Zero has the property of annihilation under multiplication. Zero, multiplied with any atom, results always and only in Zero.

`0`, or `is`, is the identity operator of the Ax automaton. It annihilates the left noun, returning the rightmost without further change.

This nomination is *consonant* with Zero's properties, considered in itself. This nomination allows the minimal triple to reduce to `0`, which is cardinal `1` of the natural numbers, a gentle mind bend called zeration.

Zeration is weird—I will grant you this. It is also necessary, and introduces our next ability, adding elements to a set in succession.

This `up` operation may be combined feasibly with `is`, thus:

```
Ξ [0 1 0 0]        →   1
```

In our first demonstration, the Zero which emerges from the reduction is the *same* Zero as found in the rightmost place of the left hand noun. In this our *second* demonstration, the One which is returned is *not* the One found in the left hand term, but the ultimate Zero, acted upon by the penultimate Zero and incremented through the `up` operator, whose effect is, to increase by One the result of Axing upon the left and right nouns. The Zero in the origin, head, or left position plays no role beyond the structural.

We clarify this with our third demonstration.

```
Ξ [0 1 0 1]        →   2
```

The Zero that became One is now One, and so that One is Two. That One is *consonant* with the quality of adding itself to things, is evident. Incrementation is the foundation of the natural numbers; the rest is induction. One is the identity of multiplication, yet it is the annihilation of nothing; we must *Ax* the left and right together, and increment upon the result.

Let us observe, also, these consonances:

1. A noun is either an atom or a cell.

2. An atom is any natural number.

3. ...

2.6.5 Branch

The study of recursive structure is called grammar. It is also of Indian invention. cgy's choice to call the noun the noun, was inspired, graceful. Calling the branch `slot`, was not.

cgy thinks of words in terms of the cost to represent them in a computation. More than four letters is profligate by this standard.[6] Be that as it may, `slot` is ugly. Recursive slot-in-slot, is not a thing. I saved four letters with `is` and `up`; I will now burn two to get six letters, for the best word for the job.[7]

Such different creatures as the deer, trees, and coral reefs, have elements we call branches. These bifurcate recursively.

```
2: A cell is an ordered pair of nouns.
```

`branch` is the first operation to require the properties of a subjective cell, in the sense that the subject must be a cell for four of the reductions to succeed. The Zero operation requires nothing at all but a noun of phrasal structure, and the status of the subject is irrelevant. One requires that the result of Axing upon

[6] Editor's note: four ASCII letters fit in one 32-bit direct atom.

[7] I believe the most important space to save is in the human mind. "Branch" is the more frequent word, and would be lower-ordered in a dictionary compression based on Zipf's Law.

the subject and object succeed, and return an atom for incrementation, but the subject may be atomic, and the returned value must be. `branch` also establishes the sense in which a pair of nouns is ordered.

We now progress in our representation. Having the ability to generate all of the natural numbers, we pat our pockets, looking for a place to put them. Thing is, they get cumbersome if we just accumulate marks. The space is linear, we would prefer logarithmic, it's more compact. Binary is the simplest scheme after unary, this is why we use it.

We will be treating repeatedly upon triple cells, which we should call a phrase. The root phrase, `Ξ [0 0 0]`, gives `0`; here Zero is the Subject, Verb, and Object of the root phrase. The `branch` operation *selects* from within the Subject, as indicated by the Object.

Which brings us to the next demonstration:

```
Ξ [2 1 2 1]        →    3
```

In which we `up Ξ [2 2 1]`, in which Two selects Two, the whole (One) of the Subject. Yielding Three, thus.

We see from this that One is the identity of the Two operation, returning the whole of the Subject. Is Zero, then, the annihilation of Two? It is precisely the inverse, and so, undefined.

Novelty is sexy. Novelty is humble. A calculation is a machine, a vessel of definite size and shape existing over a span of moments. What is above the subject, enclosing it as the subject encloses its branches?

Well, plausibly the whole of the noun, which, do what thou wilt shall be. Which is a stack overflow, basically. Or at least a no-op. So if maybe we skip that layer we might find something not interior to the noun and interiorize it. If you thought of this as an *input* I wouldn't think the less of you.

This perfectly ordinary, almost biological function, needn't be fig-leaved over by some scheme of wandering in an infinite hall of mirrors in which new nouns are sort of discovered to be already within the noun's recursive depths.

I grant this is an *option* yet it is one that leaves Two without a meaningful Zero Object. It seems wasteful, is all. We like our reductions to be compact. Consonant. Aesthetic.

2.7 The Rules of Ax

2.7.1 The First

```
Ξ [a 0 b]          →    b
```

This states the general case of the `is` identity operator. Of which no more need be said.

2.7.2 The Second

```
Ξ [a 1 0 n]        →  n + 1
```

This line is part demonstration, part rule. I believe that a concrete demonstration of the order of operation in reducing an Ax string is useful, as the pattern of first Axing the subject and object before operating upon the result is not obvious upon first appraisal.

This line is optional, a luxury, an aid to understanding.

```
Ξ [a 1 b]          →    Ξ [a b]    →    n    →    n + 1
```

Here we have the statement of the `up` operator. Which should be by this point straightforward. Note the generic character of the two signifiers `a` and `b`, and the progressive specification of `n`, which must be atomic.

2.7.3 The Third

```
Ξ [a 2 0]          →    ?
```

At last we have returned from this excursion to explanation.

As discussed, the reduction of `branch 0` is undefined. This is one of the more philosophically weighty decisions in the Ax automaton, and bears further reflection.

The property of operator `2` is that of selection. Normally this is from within the depths of the subject, which must contain all phrases necessary for the completion of the reductions specified in the object noun.

1 is chosen to represent the whole of the subject. I will here switch to the binary radix. The `10` operator, the first we express with two symbols, uses the value `1` for the whole subject, `10` for the left member, and `11` for the right. This pattern then continues, recursively, into the subject noun. We take a binary string, and consume it from the big end. When we encounter a `0`, we take the left branch, when we encounter a `1`, the right.

This is obviously the correct pattern. What could be changed about it? Each mark, be it zero or one, is a selection, and we call one left and the other right. In what sense is this meaningful?

In the sense that text flows from left to right in Latin writing. If this were in Arabic, I would hope the translator would have the good sense to call them instead right and left. We are saying 'left member' and 'right member' but we truly mean the order of sense, in which the symbols are encountered, as though we are passing through time. We might also call them the negative and positive, respectively; although Zero is not in fact negative, it is distinctive among the natural numbers for being not positive, at least, and for being as close to the negative numbers as a whole number gets. Negative and positive also are used in the sense of charge, and insofar as the 'no' and 'yes' senses of those words correspond to Boolean truth, we find the terms satisfactory on that basis. Note that we *prefer* left and right, as being legible.

This pattern, in which each bit of an atom, represented in binary and consumed from the big end, with each successive bit representing the next tier of the noun, serves as explanation for why `1` is the symbol of the topmost tier of the subject, with which `branch` is ordinarily concerned. Were it otherwise, `1` and `10` would share a tier, and that is unsatisfactory.

What then of Zero? Do we not need it? Why then do we number the operators from Zero in the first place?

Because it is primary, first of order. It is the innovation which allows us to use this binary representation, which is the minimal numeric representation which has the logarithmic properties which are sufficient to further calculation, unary being linear, which is unfeasibly wasteful in a physical calculator.

To not allow a `branch` reduction by zero, to specify that this must be an infinite loop, and state of error, is disrespectful in two ways. The first is structural; it leaves a gap, refusing to define a branch greater than itself nor fulfill its obligation to treat the natural numbers consistently. There is either a Zero or there is not, and there is.

The second is philosophical, and grounded in the concretion of an Ax automaton. There is the Ax automaton, which we are considering, but in our reality, there would be many, and each with its particular state.

It is a fact of that reality that we may wish to introduce new information into this computation, placed as the subject of further reduction. We have here a choice: we may represent this as undefined behavior, and instantiate the new noun from whatever source we've retrieved it, perhaps enumerating it into the subject of further computation, perhaps merely incorporating it into the object of calculation directly. Or we may 'discover' such new information within the subject itself, through sleight-of-hand. Such an automaton would be structured as embracing all knowledge within itself. Though this may be made to work, it is solipsistic, and we are concerned here with `10`; inside and outside is an important duality, and here, the key one.

```
Ξ [a 2 1]                  →   a
Ξ [[a b] 2 2]              →   a
Ξ [[a b] 2 3]              →   b
Ξ [a 2 (b + b)]            →   Ξ [Ξ [a 2 b] 2 2]
Ξ [a 2 (b + b + 1)]        →   Ξ [Ξ [a 2 b] 2 3]
Ξ [a 2 b]                  →   Ξ [a 2 b]
```

The remaining six reductions follow this recursive, fractal pattern of selection to its logical conclusion. The crash default is an important reduction, as it is trivial to provide `branch` with a level of detail greater than the subject contains.

Zero cannot fail. It cannot be an operator unless in the verb position of a phrase, that accomplished, it will return the object, period.

One can fail in the sense that the Axing of subject and object may not produce an atom. But this failure is in the first recursion, not in the operation of One in itself. One may be inapplicable, but given a correct reduction, it will increment the atom.

Two may fail inherently. This is worth marking with its own crash default. It is a distinctive mode of failure, much like an index error.

If the `[2 1 2 1]` demonstration were instead `[2 1 2 2]`, it would fail in the same way, by failing to reduce `[2 2 2]`, which would loop infinitely, in principle.

This first multiple reduction takes seven forms, and there are seven axiomatic operators in total. This symmetry is pleasing, and constitutes its own argument for the specific crash default and the inclusion of an undefined Zero branch.

The two recursive reductions, each singly recursive, would occur in the tail position, amenable to representation as a simple loop. Its complexity is $O(\log(n))$, formally, with the expectation that much of this can be traced away, replaced with a jump directly to the pointer for selection within the subject.

2.7.4 Distribution

The `11` operator, which we will interchangeably refer to as `3`, distributes the subject among the various objects of the computation.

This is the structural insight to which we owe Curtis Guy Yarvin our deepest respect and congratulations. I will interchangeably refer to this as the `Ax` or `Nock` operator. I trust this ambiguity will not be unduly confusing.

The insight that the concept of the 'environment' in Lisp was a harmful impediment to imposing a proper type system and functional computation is to be deeply respected. It is what enables this automaton to perform persistence and coordination of state in a repeatable, plausible fashion.

Note that `11` is consonant with the operation of taking the `branch 1`, which is the whole of the subject, and distributing it twice across the two members of the object.

Also, as an odd number, it takes a singular reduction. Lastly, it is concerned with three nouns, `a`, `b`, and `c`. We meet the first two of these these participants in the Zero reduction, one vanishing without a trace, the other carried forward. They are Axed together for the reduction of One.

The `branch` operator is concerned with a single, atomic object, which renders the choice within the subject, while the `Ax` operator concerns itself with the subject and a dual object, which is rendered into two pairings with the subject and calculated separately. Thus `11`, or `3`.

The next demonstration

```
Ξ [3 3 [[2 1] [1 2 1]] [0 2 1]]    →    [3 4]
```

combines the implicit and explicit forms of the distributive operation, splitting the atomic 3 object and incrementing the right half of this cell to produce `[3 4]`.

This is the seed of falsehood. We will discuss its significance in the next section, under equality.

When you understand, in detail, the reduction of this last demonstration, you are well on your way to understanding Ax.

Let us continue with this distributive operation, which also has a structural form, in another quiet touch of sheer brilliance.

```
Ξ [a [b c] d]     →    [Ξ [a b c] Ξ [a d]]
```

with

```
Ξ [a 3 b c]       →    Ξ [Ξ [a b] Ξ [a c]]
```

jointly manage state by consuming a chain of objects against the same context. This is the property which allows for the stack-heap duality approach to reducing by Nock a phrase, and operationally, for consistence of state along a chain of conditional operations, computation per se.

This should also render the series of operations amenable to tracing, as an optimization best applied early. Though I will note that I'm aware of no serious proposal to write one.

2.7.5 The Fourth

The test of equality is doubly recursive.

The base case of inequality between two atoms could be represented `[0 1]`. That is how I would do it. `[3 4]` has these interesting properties: it is grown, as it were, from Three, through the application of lower-ordered verbs, and contains Four, while providing a base case for the Four operation.

The base case is false, because a test of equality is concerning itself with either falsehood, or its equal and opposite, truth. As Zero is our signifier of falsehood, and is prior, the false base case is preferred.

That is, if we have two unequal atoms, this is case Zero, and reduces to Zero.

The One case is the equality of two atoms. It returns One, our symbol for Truth. Then, if we have a cell and an atom, it is definitionally false. Case `10`.

Then we must consider two cells. Recursively, by comparing the left of the left and the left of the right, and the right of the right and the right of the left, respectively. Case `11`. Closed.

We will note that Four, being even, has two reductions.

There is a trivial optimization available, if the Ax is represented using shared structure. If two pointers to cells are equal, those cells will be equal. Ax doesn't have this concept of shared structure, and inequality or equality may in any case prevail over two different pointers. It is the structure and contents of two cells, not details of their representation in memory, that are the final test.

The worst case in time complexity is $O(n)$ the size of the subjects under comparison, which can be expensive; where shared structure can be chosen, it generally should be.

2.7.6 The Fifth

The power of probability in computation is irrefutable. It is paradigmatic that it exists, in the form of novelty, a mysterious quality which influxes from the future. This stream of living energy, also called entropy, is a necessary part of computation. It is the inverse of the syntropic force necessary to physically power computation and life.

Reality itself exhibits this quality, in the form we refer to as quantum collapse. It is necessary to simulate this in a reproducible, bit-identical calculation, to model and abstract over calculations we believe to be efficient emulations of processes critical to life and intelligence.

We represent luck with the number 5. It is a coin flip, a toss of the die, a short or long straw. It is required for fair gambling and other conditions when an event's total contribution to a computation is to be distributed but not harmonically.

This Schrödinger's bit we call 'Red'. A difference between `branch 0` and the `flip` operation is that the former may return anything at all, hopefully well-formed, while the latter must return either `0` or `1`. Deriving this bit from a high-quality physical source of entropy cannot be compelled. It is highly recommended.

In cryptography, Red bits derive their value from being unknown outside the computation. The simplest cryptographic scheme, the one-time pad, is simply shared entropy, XORed across the secret, consuming the entropy by contaminating it with a pattern. Although I have a question about that last part, which keeps me up at night. It should be the subject of another, shorter, and later, thesis.

For probabilistic programming generally, it is the quality of being unpredictable that is valued. Both of these can be obtained, because the physical world allows for processes which are chaotic, unpredictable even across a short term.

It is important to stress that the quality of novelty is particular and exists precisely in its unpredictable nature. If a computation is to be repeated, the choice must be made to either follow the path laid down by the previous ingression of novelty, or to discard it, in favor of a new path, perhaps more pleasing in some quality. Perhaps not.

It is certainly possible to choose to represent only deterministic calculations, or worse, to treat entropy as a class of discovered information, delivered on a card like anything else. This underestimates its importance. It is Axiomatic that a 5 will return a fair toss, an implementation that cannot provide this feature on command is a failing case of an Ax machine. `/dev/random` is not optional. You can, of course, dummy it up and/or replay it, as long as you know what you're doing. It's your Ax, dude, jam on it.

The engineers building immense tensor math rigs for various forms of machine learning are basically taking a GPU (this works because the math needed to simulate reality is the math needed to simulate reality) and attaching an entropic firehose to it. They might be beefing it up with some pseudorandom tumbling scheme, I consider this bad engineering but I could get talked out of the insistence on just setting up a circuit with good noisy properties and listening in.[8]

Five's cardinal connection with this action is best inferred by contemplating coordinates as `0` in the identity/origin position, `1` as extension, `2` as rotation, and `3` and `4` as the repetition of extension and rotation. The group produced in this manner is thus far deterministic, in that one would call in all cases the positive and negative vectors of the extensions positive and negative, and the rotations deosil and widdershins, or dextro- and laevo-, or what have you, understanding that the head is the positive terminal; but upon reaching the fifth, third extension, which creates space as generally experienced, we are impelled to make a choice. One choice of positivity creates a right-handed structure of coordination, the other, left-handed. This chirality is therefore associated with choice, and choice's cousin, luck.

A coin flip is a forced choice, distinguished from a free choice, which is more normal when benefits and costs are clear.

We place the Red bit in the `11` position of the subject, in consonance with the odd nature of these two numbers. Also in our belief that the senseward side corresponds with the future, as novelty does as well.

There remains, axiomatically, one operation, corresponding to the third, and last possible, rotation in space.

---

[8] I don't know about the rest of you, but if I'm going to employ probabilistic inference to ride some kind of Stephensonesque articulated chevalier, I'd like the activation thresholds to actually be driven by physically-generated randomness. Not that I have concrete plans, I'd just like to, eventually. Batteries are only getting smarter.

I did spend a few months insisting that `flip`, until very recently `fuzz`, be based on atomic decay, entirely, and was talked down. I do try to listen when others are speaking.

2.7.7 Cell

`cell` is a simple enough operation. One simply is or one isn't. Our reality exhibits cellularity at several scales, including several at the seductively and subjectively interesting biological level.[9]

We represent the test for this quality with the number Six. Six is the smallest number which is perfect. Six has the pleasing property of being composable as 2 by 3, or 3 by 2. These representing the interesting classes of cells, which we could call the structural and the phrasal. Geometrically, six circles fit tangent to each other around a seventh circle of the same size, these numbers being twelve and thirteenth in the case of spheres.

Let me stress that those pairs of numbers, the cardinal latter a double of the cardinal first, are the same member expressed cardinally and ordinarily.

The sixfold harmony of the circle around itself has been associated with the angel Metatron since Antiquity. It is basic

[9]To sketch those which make up a human, there are the subatomic, atomic, molecular, nuclear, cellular, organic, and personal, each exhibiting the common property of compactness and containment around a center.

After that, the extended phyla or clades of our biological kingdom have, despite surprising amounts of lateral transfer, a basically tree-like structure, with more general common ancestors encompassing more specific and more recent beings. As family is both the description for the most differentiated and specific multi-person entity, and a word used higher in the tree for a much more extensive grouping, I would call these cellular groupings familial.

I say our kingdom, and observe the plant kingdom shares our proclivities, while the Archaea, Procaryotes, Eucaryotes, and Fungi seem more web-like in their association. Fungal reproduction is particularly... weird in that regard. Intricate, would be a good word, rhyme's with Indra's Net. Virally-mediated lateral transfer is resisted by our kingdom, but so is polyploidy, and both happen from time to time.

We are unique among our kingdom for having almost a second form of life, certainly a secondary identity, which is ultimately linguistic in setting the boundaries of cellularity, which might be summed as the shibboleths of shared understanding. The tribes, clubs or parties, egregores, corporations, cultures, and nations, formed by this common association, often form among those kindred of ancestry, but also often, divide us differently from the forms of our physical inheritance.

Surely we may count above those the planet we inhabit, its Solar System, our Galaxy, and, multicellular and irregular in shape though they be, the galactic cluster, followed, ultimately as far as we know, by the Universe.

to our experience of geometry as living beings, as Buckminster Fuller extensively and with great idiom discusses in Synergetics. That circularity is suggestive of cellularity I take as an evident fact.

Note that, once more, an even rule has two reductions. This is not a coincidence, because nothing is ever a coincidence.

With this, the seventh of the axiomatic operations, numbered Six, we have a total; these are the operations collectively necessary to a well-formed automaton. Upon these we may rest a further foundation.

2.7.8 Compose

cgy wrote the idioms. I've adopted them, as sensible extensions. In this instance, our assignment of number is identical.

```
Ξ [a 7 b c]          →     Ξ [a 3 b 0 c]
```

This uses the `Nock` operation to distribute the subject across an object, `b`, subsequently providing this reduction as the subject of another phrase.

As an odd reduction, there is only the one way to do it. Let's look again at the last demonstration:

```
Ξ [3 3 [[2 1] [1 2 1]] [0 2 1]]    →    [3 4]
```

Function composition is inevitable in the Ax automaton, but worthwhile of marking, as higher operations are assuredly built upon it. We actually intend to follow this basic scheme well past the lemmas, through dictionary compression, assignment of an ordinal, and compilation of the elided strings. The result is simply run in its complex form, enriched with information we can extract during compilation.

Which may still be optimized further through tracing. Giving distinct operations distinct identities, assigning verbs in a useful order, can only aid this operation, which consists in its essence of eliminating any step in a reduction which doesn't advance a mutation present in the final state.

2.7.9 If

It is canonical to test for the truth of a condition, performing the left or first portion of a calculation if it succeeds, the right otherwise.

Though it can't affect correctness, it is a waste of energy to calculate the unchosen path. This requires `if` to be a 'special form' in Lisp dialects, which have the additional problem of side effects, making this a requirement, not just a good idea.. In Ax it can be written as a simple term rewrite, with the unchosen condition discarded by branching on the choice of c or d. Instead I have chosen to incorporate this object annihilation as a direct reduction.

```
Ξ [a 8 b c d]      →      Ξ [a b] → 1 → Ξ [a c]
Ξ [a 8 b c d]      →      Ξ [a b] → 0 → Ξ [a d]
```

Eight is 2 raised to the 3rd power. It is in that sense, selective distribution across only one of two objects, the other annihilated.

The decision to use a true Boolean, refusing to reduce an `8` which does not resolve `Ξ [a b]` as either a `1` or `0`, was ultimately guided by the low-ordering instinct. We don't yet have a test of relative atomic order, and when we do, it's not a hard problem to make that itself return `0` or `1`.

2.7.10 Extend

Again the name was chosen by cgy, who identified the pattern. The tenth operation, represented as 9, this can also be written as a macro:

```
Ξ [a 9 b c]          →      Ξ [a 7 [[7 [2 1] b] 2 1] c]
```

To quote ... the author "[this] is `7`, except that the subject for `c` is not simply the product of `b`, but the ordered pair of the product of `b` and the original subject."

```
Ξ [3 3 [[2 1] [1 2 1]] [0 2 1]]    →    [3 4]
```

does not emulate this precisely, but the effect is much the same. I'm not sure I like the placement of the intermediate product at 2 and the subject at 3. It feels backwards, insofar as the subject already existed and its new addition was just created, left is temporally before right when these words are used in their senseward, rather than their chiral, senses. So we should prefer an order.

2.7.11 Hint

This is a set of two expansions which do nothing, each in its own way.[10] The Nock automaton takes a firm stance that neither input nor output are to be handled at the bottom layer.[11]

This means that information is discovered within the subject on 'cards', acted upon, and then cards are 'released' into the wild, exiting the computation. The Ten operation, which shares its place in Nock and Ax, is not there used for this later 'releasing'. Instead it is used for 'hinting', a peculiar custom relating to jetting, which is not, peculiar that is, when you realize it's the familiar foreign function interface with a requirement that you write the entire library in the slow language as well. Jit and Jet are also caught by the pin-pen merger, which is droll.

It is the hinting itself I deem unnecessary, if we simply continue the pattern which is becoming clear in the Idioms and is spelled out more explicitly in the Lemmas. That is ordinary dictionary compression; we proceed to assign natural numbers to particular nouns we encounter during compilation, save those nouns as the contents of the dictionary, and design and run the compressed Ax code directly, without bothering to consult the dictionary as to the definitive meaning, just a jump table (you knew it was a `vtable`). The dictionary's structural representation as an Ax noun could be as simple as an ordered list, if we wish it to be compact, or we could construct a balanced representation if we find ourselves consulting it frequently.

A custom of using such a dictionary is somewhat metacircular, as you'd build it in the higher-level language, thereby establishing structural requirements for decoding the dictionary itself. But this is necessary anyway in establishing the

[10] Editor's note: to wit, the hint operator, opcode 11 in Nock 4K.

[11] Ultimately this is because down that road lie Monads, and if you don't fear and distrust monads in 2017 I wish I shared your jaunty mien.

next layer of abstraction. It does not increase the complexity of the Ax spec, following its spirit as well as its letter by simply continuing to build operations in the now familiar way.

These cannot be universal, or maybe they can be; for my part, I view the Lemmas as sharing some of the inevitable nature of correspondence, but not so much that I would want to continue down that path further.

What then do we wish for Ten? Let us view it:

```
Ξ [a 10 b c]          →    Ξ [a c]
Ξ [a 10 [b c] d]      →    Ξ [a 9 c 7 [2 3] d]
```

We see that the first just annihilates `b`. It's like the reverse of `0`, which is pleasant, as the second place in the decimal system where the Zero appears.[12] As is proper to any operation ending in `0`, it has two reductions. The second does `Ξ [b c]` and discards it, moving on to `Ξ [a d]`. So what's useful about this? This could cause a side-effect, like printing a variable.

I would think it more proper to make more use of Ten, the `toss` operator. In particular I might want `b` in the first reduction to resolve undefined behavior along `branch 0` of another Ax computation, building thereby an Axtor model of cooperative behavior between small, well-defined, predictable computers.[13]

2.8 Invocation

Hail Muse! Be merciful,
In bending our arc toward beauty.

The `11` operator describes what Hoon calls a 'core'.

```
Ξ [a 11 b c]          →    Ξ [a 7 c 3 [2 1] 2 b]
```

[12]In binary it is `1010`, which is pretty neat actually, it's like `10` is O-10, if a Japanese-'Arabic' (Hindu) construction may be indulged. *Oh-ten-sei.*

[13]The tenth Sephiroth is Malkuth, the Kingdom. This is where another, denser layer of reality begins in the ladder-like Tree of Life. I think this reflects the Phoenician/Canaanite/Hebrew (these terms are somewhat but not completely interchangeable) alphabet, where the first nine marks are 1-9, the next ten are 10-90, and then we get some number of marks in the 100 series as well.

Now I think this is a pretty macro, with that `3 2 1` streak in it. Are we still in the realm of inevitability?

The cardinal properties of numbers become more complex, as a rule, as they get further from the origin. For instance a number with many prime factors has qualities specific to each of those factors, and each of their combinations.

Eleven has the virtue of being prime, at least. It is the last of our five Idioms. cgy stops counting at 10, leaving him with 11 operations in total. Thanks to our lucky `flip` operation, we have 12 total, which must enumerate to 11, sure as you're born. I'll just say it's unclear what's inevitable. I'm pretty sure `9` is backward and it may get stuck that way. `11` is even harder to make a case for, I guess, but trace it, it's a good reduction.

2.9 Lemmas

I include the Lemmas for two reasons. The first is to provide for the operations on natural numbers I consider basic. The cell is of much more recent innovation, and being protean and multiple, of an entirely different order of complexity, at least to a human mind. The two words 'natural numbers' bring in a huge amount of prior art, and this assuredly includes things like comparison and division, and yes, I consider modulus more basic than power, which compounds through repetition an operation that is already compounded through repetition, while cyclic arithmetic is the basis of everything recurrent in a regular or harmonic way. It belongs after division, which must have two reductions to forbid zero, because modulus completes division by providing the remainder.

The second is to indicate the path forward. Ax as a compiler target with a dictionary assembled from foreign function interfaces written in a language which expects to be represented on an Ax-class automaton. Multiplication being 15, 31 might be a nice spot on the shelf for power, might not. At some point we want to start organizing by common utility, in the familiar library pattern.

That's Hoon, basically. At first, and rebuilt utterly below C level.

References

Buswell, Ben (2010). “Undefined Intimacy With the Machine: Standard C and ‘Undefined Behavior’.” In: *Critical Code Studies 2010 Conference Proceedings.* URL: `http://thoughtmesh.net/publish/367.php` (visited on ~2024.1.25).

~sorreg-namtyv, Curtis Yarvin (2010) “Maxwell’s Equations of Software”. URL: `https://www.unqualified-reservations.org/2010/01/maxwells-equations-of-software/` (visited on ~2025.8.28).

A noun is an atom or a cell. An atom is a natural number.
A cell is an ordered pair of nouns.

Reduce by the first matching pattern; variables match any noun.

```
nock(a)             *a
[a b c]             [a [b c]]

?[a b]              0
?a                  1
+[a b]              +[a b]
+a                  1 + a
=[a a]              0
=[a b]              1

/[1 a]              a
/[2 a b]            a
/[3 a b]            b
/[(a + a) b]        /[2 /[a b]]
/[(a + a + 1) b]    /[3 /[a b]]
/a                  /a

#[1 a b]            a
#[(a + a) b c]      #[a [b /[(a + a + 1) c]] c]
#[(a + a + 1) b c]  #[a [/[(a + a) c] b] c]
#a                  #a

*[a [b c] d]        [*[a b c] *[a d]]

*[a 0 b]            /[b a]
*[a 1 b]            b
*[a 2 b c]          *[*[a b] *[a c]]
*[a 3 b]            ?*[a b]
*[a 4 b]            +*[a b]
*[a 5 b c]          =[*[a b] *[a c]]

*[a 6 b c d]        *[a *[[c d] 0 *[[2 3] 0 *[a 4 4 b]]]]
*[a 7 b c]          *[*[a b] c]
*[a 8 b c]          *[[*[a b] a] c]
*[a 9 b c]          *[*[a c] 2 [0 1] 0 b]
*[a 10 [b c] d]     #[b *[a c] *[a d]]

*[a 11 [b c] d]     *[[*[a c] *[a d]] 0 3]
*[a 11 b c]         *[a c]

*a                  *a
```

www.ingramcontent.com/pod-product-compliance
Lightning Source LLC
LaVergne TN
LVHW040514210926
848480LV00005BA/1462